Film and Television Distribution and the Internet

To my wife Fadime and daughter Melike-Grace,
my mother Muriel and all my family.

Film and Television Distribution and the Internet

A Legal Guide for the Media Industry

ANDREW SPARROW

GOWER

Published by
Gower Publishing Limited
Gower House
Croft Road
Aldershot
Hampshire GU11 3HR
England

Ashgate Publishing Company
Suite 420
101 Cherry Street
Burlington, VT 05401-4405
USA

Andrew Sparrow has asserted his moral right under the Copyright, Designs and Patents Act, 1988, to be identified as the author of this work.

British Library Cataloguing in Publication Data
Sparrow, Andrew
    Film and television distribution and the Internet : a legal
    guide for the media industry
    1. Motion pictures - Distribution - Law and legislation
    2. Television programs - Syndication - Law and legislation
    3. Internet 4. Copyright - Motion pictures 5. Copyright -
    Broadcasting rights
    I. Title
    343'.0787914

    ISBN-13: 9780566087363

Library of Congress Cataloging-in-Publication Data
Sparrow, Andrew.
Film and television distribution and the Internet : a legal guide for the media industry / by Andrew Sparrow.
        p. cm.
    Includes bibliographical references and index.
    ISBN 978-0-566-08736-3
1. Mass media--Law and legislation--European Union countries. 2. Electronic commerce--Law and legislation--European Union countries. 3. Video rental services--Law and legislation--European Union countries. 4. Motion pictures--Internet marketing--Law and legislation--European Union countries. 5. Television programs--Internet marketing--Law and legislation--European Union countries. 6. Copyright and electronic data processing--European Union countries.
    I. Title.

    KJE6946.S68 2007
    343.2409'9--dc22

                                                                    2007003899

Printed and bound in Great Britain by TJ International Ltd, Padstow, Cornwall.

Contents

About the Author

Andrew Sparrow is a national award winning Solicitor and founder of Lecote Solicitors, a niche commercial law firm concentrating on internet, new media and IT law.

He was one of the first solicitors in the United Kingdom to recognise and pursue the legal issues relating to online business. Andrew is author of several books on commercial and internet law published internationally.

In a national poll conducted in 2004 and supported by the Department of Trade and Industry he was acknowledged as one of 100 individuals in the United Kingdom who have contributed most to the development of the internet in the last ten years.

He can be contacted at:

Lecote Solicitors
New Broad Street House
35 New Broad Street
London
EC2M 1NH
Tel: 020 7194 7705
Email: Law@lecote.com
www.lecote.com

CHAPTER 1

The Impact of the Internet on Film and Television Distribution

It is hard to imagine that, as late as 2005, at least two-thirds of all independent film distribution deals did not account for internet rights. Such rights went unrealised and were licensed as part of all-rights packages or bundled within the video or television deal. That position is now changing as it is recognised that, for the first time, the internet provides filmmakers with the means of distribution as well as the means of production. Moreover, they can interact directly with their target audience. The internet extends the range of what we think of as filmmaking. It has taken more than a decade for the internet to find a role as a commercial medium with a meaningful impact on the film and television industries. In that time a communications revolution has penetrated the day-to-day operations of industry all over the world and afforded individuals with access to information hitherto unobtainable. There are now close to a billion people with access to the internet.

In the last decade a number of now household names have proved the efficacy of the internet for business. Amazon spawned a revolution in book retailing and created a paradigm for consumer purchases of books, DVDs and CDs which others have since followed. Easyjet led the way in the use of the internet for flight reservations and, through the cost savings achieved by use of the web, also developed the low cost airline model which is now a part of the commercial aviation industry. In 2005 Google was the highest valued media company in the world. Yahoo has around 400 million users per month. YouTube has taken even new media experts by surprise in terms of its hugely successful online video file sharing service. To say that the internet has changed our way of life is no understatement.

Digital technology enables information, software, text, pictures and, importantly, films to be copied millions of times without loss of quality, downloaded without the knowledge of the copyright holder and transmitted around the world instantly over networks. Traditional models for film distribution are being overturned. Faced with an ever wider array of on-demand and sell-through delivery mechanisms it is vital that content owners exercise more control over their distribution destinies.

Whilst the fortunes of the internet's commercial career have fluctuated, the legal issues surrounding internet business have always been founded on an essential need to safeguard the interests of all who use the medium.

The law relating to internet film and television distribution is complex. There is hardly an aspect of internet film promotion, sale and distribution which does not have a legal dimension. It will be seen that the majority of the law in this field has been introduced very recently. Such is the process of legal development that legislation must be interpreted by the courts to establish how it impacts on specific facts. This is the preserve of case law. Given the short time since the introduction of the variety of legislation, at the time of writing there is very little case law precedent. Undoubtedly it will develop in the coming years.

The problem facing lawmakers in the digital era is the sheer pace of development. The dynamics of the technology are changing very rapidly and the law must constantly adapt to the continuing stream of innovation. This presents difficulties because, whilst it is recognised that the internet will continue to advance, one cannot be certain of the direction the new media industry is taking and which services will become widespread. There are some indicators. Patterns of internet use are emerging. Most people use their computer at home for internet access. The evidence suggests the PC is moving from the bedroom to the living room and it is gradually competing for attention with the television. Forecasts predict that half of all mobile phone users in Europe will subscribe to a 3G service by 2010. Video downloading is expected to account for approximately one-third of the downloading market by 2011.[1] By that year it is believed that Internet Protocol Television (IPTV) revenues will rise to £6.4 billion worldwide and there will be 36 million IPTV homes.[2] Current analysis has revealed that following five years of double digit growth, the retail DVD market tumbled into sharp decline in 2005 as consumers lost interest in collecting DVDs.

It all points to one thing. The opportunity for the film and television industries to offer content direct to internet and mobile phone audiences is huge.

---

1   Verdict Research, 2006: http://www.verdict.co.uk/.
2   Informa Research, 2006: http://www.informa.com/.

This book is written for those industries or anyone associated with them. Whether they be studios, broadcasters, sales agents, distributors, Internet Service Providers, film financiers, online film retailers or lawyers wishing to gain an insight into the subject, all should find the work useful. Practical advice is given on how to approach key relationships with Internet Service Providers, content aggregators and the consumer who downloads film and television output. The law is explained in straightforward terms and applied throughout in a media business context. It is hoped the reader will gain a good understanding of the legal issues in the rapidly expanding, constantly evolving and fascinating world of internet film and television.

CHAPTER 2

Online Contracts for the Sale of Film Titles and Merchandise

One of the features of new media is that there are multiple audiences. From video-on-demand cable services to download-to-own services, this is an exciting period of change for the film and television media industries. It is also an opportunity for content providers previously shut out of potential markets by the so-called gatekeepers or intermediaries. With the internet it is more than ever possible for the film to find its audience and that audience, as will be discussed elsewhere in this book, can be very precisely targeted.

Music retailers and record industry suppliers may have been slow to adapt to the world of internet music but at the time of writing the music industry is quickly taking advantage of the flexibility and low scale-up costs of digital music. The film industry is now facing the same issues for film content, although with the benefit of the music industry's experience. In addition, there are still issues around the speed of film downloads, for example, and the differing nature of music and film content – one (music) requiring passive listening thereby increasing the range apparatus through which it might be enjoyed, the other (film) demanding a more focused effort.

There is a transformation taking place in the way in which people interact with film and television. Those with broadband connections use the internet more than they watch television, while young people familiar with sophisticated mobile phones are much more receptive to the possibility of watching television on the phone in the future. New services present new market opportunities for the film business. Nonetheless, whatever format is used transacting business over the internet requires the formation of legally binding contracts. The issue of how a contract comes into existence when dealing online is one which, from the first stirrings of e-commerce, attracted significant legal attention. There had to be an ability for website operators and their visitors to enter into binding legal relations. However, it was also clear that the very nature of the internet would present a raft of new legal problems. Which country's law would apply to this global medium? At what point would a contract come into existence? These questions were resolved and are reviewed in this book. However, to understand how a film business can operate safely online it is necessary to consider how English law approaches the matter of contract formation generally. This is because these long-established legal principles apply to internet trade and shape the way which websites must be configured. In this section we will examine these contract law considerations and see how a contract can be made over the internet and by mobile phone text messaging.

The assertion by Bill Gates in his book *The Road Ahead*[1] that the internet would carry us into a new world of low friction and low overhead capitalism, in which market information would be plentiful and transaction costs low, has proved correct. It is this characteristic which is now exercising the minds of those in the film industry. The access to online film files is limitless and vast databases of film works can be maintained. The films can be distributed without the need for physical dispatch, thus making transaction costs almost non-existent. The internet represents a triumph of technology over the constraints which hitherto prevented instantaneous communication on a truly global scale.

As the medium thus fits within an established legal framework, so it is necessary to understand the process of contract formation. Such an appreciation is critical to online business, since the sheer openness of the system can cause problems.

ENGLISH CONTRACT LAW

English law requires a number of things to happen before it can be said that a legally binding contract has been formed. A contract is founded on agreement. In its purest form agreement arises from offer and acceptance. One person makes an offer, another person accepts that offer. However, to constitute a legally enforceable contract the law demands four elements. They are:

- offer;

- acceptance;

- consideration (usually payment);

- an intention to create legal relations.

In this chapter we will consider the concept of an offer as well as another important issue for proper contract formation, that of the capacity of those under 18 to enter into contracts.

---

[1]   William H. Gates, with Nathan Myhrvold and Peter Rinearson (1995), *The Road Ahead* (New York: Viking Penguin).

OFFER

An offer is a proposition put by one person (or persons) to another person (or persons) coupled with an intimation that he or she is willing to be bound to that proposition. The offeror – that is, the person who makes the offer – may make his or her offer to a particular person or to a group of persons or, as in the context of the internet, to the entire world.

He or she may make this offer in writing, in spoken words or by conduct. The first two can be grasped immediately and the written contract often takes the form of an elaborate document with numerous clauses and sub-clauses. How can conduct create an offer? Well, an everyday act of conduct which constitutes an offer can be found in a bus driver pulling up at a bus stop.

The intimation that the offeror is willing to be bound need not be stated in words, be they written or spoken. It may be, and frequently is, inferred from the nature of the offeror's proposition or from the circumstances in which the proposition is made.

When you make an offer, you are expressing a desire to enter into a contract based on specified terms and conditions on the understanding that if the other party accepts it the agreement will be legally binding.

Offers can be made using virtually any form of communication. Over the years, as new means of communication developed, the courts have had to establish how contracts were to be formed by the use of developing mediums, from simple letter post to the advent of the telephone, fax machine and now e-mail, SMS text and, of course, over the internet.

It is vital to consider this legal explanation of what constitutes an 'offer'. English law states that if a reasonable person would interpret a particular action or communication as an offer (a readiness to bind oneself), it is an offer whether the party intended it or not. It is therefore the appearance of an offer that is more important than actual intent. It can be seen that this is where the danger to electronic business exists. Careless online statements or poorly constructed websites could amount to a film business making unintentional offers to the world that could result in unwanted binding legal contracts once consumers accept.

OFFER DISTINGUISHED FROM INVITATION TO TREAT

There is a concept in English contract law which at first hearing sounds odd but which is necessary in the sales environment and is actually central to website commercial dealings. It is necessary to distinguish a true offer from an 'invitation to treat'. The importance of the distinction is that if a true offer is made and is then accepted, the offeror is bound.

Conversely, if what the offeror said or did is not a true offer but merely an invitation to treat, the other person cannot, by saying 'I accept', bind the offeror and thus create a contract. Important though this distinction is, it is not always easy to make.

The contrast between the two principles can best be illustrated by the use of examples common to commercial life. First, the tender situation. Here, the distinction between an offer and an invitation to treat is reasonably clearly seen. If a company asks a number of suppliers to put in tenders for supplying it with some particular goods or services, the company is not thereby making an offer to those suppliers. Consequently, the company is not bound to accept the lowest or any other tender. It is not the company that makes the offer; the offer comes from the supplier in the form of a tender or estimate.

The next example of an invitation to treat is the display of articles on shelves in a shop, for example, DVDs. The offer is not made by the shop owner. They are only making an invitation to treat. The offer is in fact made by the customer taking the DVD to the cash desk and tendering money to purchase. That offer by the customer can then be accepted or refused by the shop. The courts take the same view of goods displayed in a shop window.

The same rule applies to an advertisement placed, for example, by a company stating that it is willing to sell DVDs. The general rule is that an advertisement is not an offer, merely an invitation to treat. We consider advertisements in the context of the internet in Chapter 12.

For the online film business to protect itself from making unintentional offers, it needs to observe the fine distinction between an offer and an invitation.

The internet uses modern digital technology and ordinary telephone lines. It is not a closed system like telex and it offers much more through its interconnecting networks. Anyone with a modern computer, a modem, suitable programs and a paid-up subscription to an Internet Service Provider can gain access to the system. By means of that system, a user can obtain information from websites, send messages through e-mail, and order merchandise and services.

A contract need not be a detailed formal document. It is possible to form a legally recognised contract by the simple exchange of e-mail. There might be arguments over uncertainty of terms and perhaps the court might refuse to confirm a contract if there are so many aspects of the purported agreement unclear to make the contract void for uncertainty. Nonetheless, e-mail exchange can create legal relations, so care must be taken. A contract can also be formed by mobile phone SMS. An exchange of text messages could constitute a contract between the parties.

FILM WEBSITES

A website operated by a film company is the electronic equivalent of a shop window. Similarly, e-mail price lists for film merchandise, for example, are analogous to circulars in conventional commerce. The better view is that a website constitutes an invitation to treat by its form rather than an offer for sale. However, that is not implied by law.

It is important that the film company makes it clear that its website does not constitute an irrevocable offer for sale of the film content or merchandise made available or services detailed on the site. To minimise the risk the film website and e-mail solicitations should have disclaimers explicitly defining them to be invitations to treat and not offers.

If one considers the issue, if the content of the film company website constitutes an offer then the business will have no control over who it becomes legally bound to. This would be a commercially intolerable scenario. By the inclusion of an appropriate disclaimer it will ensure that it has the ability to select customers and manage its supply of content, merchandise or services.

For many reasons the film company may not wish to deal with all consumers from all jurisdictions across the world. The website might be targeted to specific audiences and it is common for film companies to operate various websites if the company is international, perhaps with one site covering Europe and another governing the US market. Thus it is important for a film company to retain the power to accept or refuse. In this way it can decline online customers without the fear of being in breach of contract.

In fact, if the film company only ever intends to accept orders from say, UK-based film-buying consumers, since the internet is a global medium it must place a notice on its website stating that the contents of its website are for UK customers only.

DISCLAIMERS AND EXCLUSION CLAUSES

We are all familiar with clauses in contracts that seek to restrict or limit a company's legal liability in certain situations. A disclaimer or exemption clause is a term in a contract that seeks to exempt one of the parties from liability in certain events. The same principles apply to what are called limitation clauses. These are clauses that attempt to limit, rather than wholly exclude, a party's liability. An example is a clause that states that complaints must be made within a certain period of time.

An exemption clause is a perfectly legitimate device in contracts between parties of equal bargaining power. In general, the courts will regard two businesses who wish to enter into a contract as having equal bargaining power. Clearly, there are in reality significant differences in commercial strength between businesses and many commercial dealings are entered into on terms favourable to the stronger party. That is simple commercial reality. Broadly, though, the law treats both businesses as having a greater understanding of commercial transactions than, say, the individual consumer. If a company therefore strikes a bad commercial bargain with another company the courts will not intervene for that reason alone. One of the reasons why a film company should understand all the issues covered in this book is that such understanding ought to help them to avoid entering into a commercial agreement with another business on terms unfavourable to the film company.

However, where the parties are unequal exclusion clauses might create injustice. The law will regard a business and a consumer as unequal parties: the business is treated as the dominant party. In the UK, as indeed throughout the EU, consumers are afforded considerable protection when dealing with businesses. It is that policy which dictates much of the law relating to online sales to consumers and which we consider in this book in a variety of contexts.

Online consumer trade has seen huge growth in recent years, particularly for items such as flight bookings, hotel bookings and the purchasing of books, CDs and DVDs. The acquisition of film content via the internet has also found its market. In respect of online contracts made under English law, and in particular contracts made with consumers, the film company, as supplier of merchandise or services, will need to take into account the provisions of various relevant statutes.

As stated, the law assumes that consumers deserve greater legal protection. Clearly, this distinction is relevant in the online and mobile phone environment. It is essential that the film company appreciates who its website is targeted towards, as this will determine the nature and extent of the online legal terms and conditions it may post on its website. In Chapter 3 we examine some examples of online terms and conditions.

A number of Acts of Parliament and European Regulations have been developed which are designed to give the consumer protection. It is useful to consider these briefly. These laws are not written for internet trade alone but have particular relevance to e-commerce.

The Consumer Credit Act 1974

This Act regulates the content of agreements for the provision of credit, sets out various procedures which must be followed to protect consumers and establishes a regime for licensing businesses which provide consumer credit or consumer hire. As a result of changes made to the legislation, the provision of consumer credit online to UK consumers is now permitted.

The Consumer Protection Act 1987

This Act imposes strict liability in certain circumstances on the manufacturer (and others in the distribution chain) of defective goods which cause death or personal injury or loss or damage to property.

The Unfair Terms in Consumer Contracts Regulations 1994

These Regulations came into force on 1 July 1995. They give effect to a European Community Directive (93/13/EEC) to promote harmonisation of the laws of member states so as to ensure that contracts with consumers do not include terms that are unfair to the consumer. They apply to standard contracts entered into between the sellers or suppliers of goods or services to consumers. They introduce a general concept of 'unfairness' in terms. Essentially, the contract terms are subject to a test of fairness. If they are regarded as unfair they will be of no legal effect. If such terms are unfair then under Regulation 5(1) 'they shall not be binding on the consumer'. The definition of a consumer under the Regulations is quite wide. Regulation 2(1) defines a consumer as a 'natural person who, in making a contract to which these Regulations apply, is acting for purposes which are outside his business'. This definition includes small business persons for activities which are incidental to their business.

The Unfair Contract Terms Act 1977 (as amended) ('UCTA')

This is the Act which dominates exclusion and limitation clauses and how they are to be regarded at law. The Act applies to film company legal terms imposed on consumers. It also applies to internet sales of film and merchandise.

It is first necessary to study two definitions in the Act. First, 'business liability' and second, 'deals as consumer'. Most of the Act applies only to business liability and the consumer has a specially favoured status under the legislation.

'Business liability' is liability arising from things done by a person in the course of business or from the occupation of business premises. A person 'deals as consumer' if he or she does not make the contract in the course of a business and the other party does make the contract in the course of a business.

If the contract is for the supply of goods, there is an additional point, namely that the goods must be of a type ordinarily supplied for private use or consumption.

Business liability for death or personal injury resulting from negligence cannot be excluded or restricted by any contract term or notice. In the case of other loss or damage, a film company cannot so exclude or restrict its business liability for negligence except insofar as the terms or notice satisfies the requirement of reasonableness.

The requirement of reasonableness is that the term shall be a fair and reasonable one to be included, having regard to all the circumstances which were, or ought to have been, known to or in the contemplation of the parties when the contract was made.

The Act lays down guidelines for the application of the reasonableness test. So, when one party deals as consumer or on the film company's standard written terms of business the film company cannot:

- when it is in breach of contract, exclude or restrict its business liability in respect of the breach;

- claim to be entitled to render a contractual performance substantially different from that which was reasonably expected of it;

- claim to be entitled to render no performance at all except in all three cases subject to the requirement of reasonableness.

CAPACITY

Under English law of contract, people below the age of majority – which is 18 – are called minors (children). The law is based on two principles. The first is that the law must protect the child against his or her inexperience, which may enable an adult to take unfair advantage of him or her or to induce him or her to enter into an contract which is improvident. This principle is on the basis of the general rule that a child is not bound by his or her contracts. The second principle is that the law should not cause unnecessary hardship to adults who deal fairly with children. Under this principle certain contracts with children are valid.

It is beyond the scope of this book to examine the various situations where contracts can be upheld against children, as we are only concerned with the online world.

A useful example of how the problem of contracting with children can arise in the context of internet and mobile phone communications lies in the 'Crazy Frog' ringtone. In 2005 a company called Jamster, which sells ringtones for mobile phones, flooded television commercial breaks with advertisements which featured an animated amphibian in a leather motorcycle cap and goggles. The character was supported by a music accompaniment which most people found annoying. The advertising campaign was hugely successful. The music track topped the UK charts and sales of the ringtone version also represented a major commercial success. The Advertising Standards Authority received several complaints about the campaign, but the real cause for concern lay in the alleged misleading promotion of the ringtone. This led to complaints being laid before the Independent Committee for the Supervision of Standards of Telephone Information Services (ICSTIS). It received over 100 complaints from people who thought they had bought the ringtone at a price of £3 only to find that they had also unwittingly signed up for a subscription service costing £3 per week. Many of the subscribers were children and the error was only discovered when parents received their phone bill.

CHECKLIST

- Ensure by including in the website terms and conditions that the existence of the film website is expressed to be an invitation to treat and not an offer for sale of the items made available through it.

- Only include exclusion or limitation clauses in online contract terms which are reasonable, whether dealing with consumers or other businesses.

- Exercise caution if targeting the online service towards young people and be mindful of the legal capacity laws.

CHAPTER 3

Website Terms and Conditions for the Supply of Film DVDs and Other Film Merchandise over the Internet

HOW TO ENSURE THE LEGAL TERMS GOVERN THE CONTRACT

In this section we will review the principal terms and conditions which should operate to govern the online sale of physical products typically offered by film companies and associated businesses over the internet. This might include the sale of promotional material. As throughout this book, we will use the term 'film company', which might be a production company, sales agent, film distributor or any other business associated with the promotion, retail or distribution of film content. For convenience of description we will simply use this generic term.

In Chapter 6 we examine the huge importance of marketing a film title and the merchandise that surrounds the title. The film company has to reach out to its e-mail database and find its audience online. Film company websites are growing in sophistication, as is the range of services they typically offer. The more successful a film is the more likely it is that filmgoers will want to buy products that provide more information about the title and its stars, for example, behind-the-scenes footage and interviews with the cast. They will buy merchandise such as model toys, posters, screensavers and clothing items. They will also want to purchase branded products such as food, drinks and sweets. Consumers generally are spending more than ever online and so the internet is a vital tool for film companies.

The manner in which merchandise must be made available to website visitors is prescribed by a variety of laws which many film companies might not appreciate.

We have seen in Chapter 2 the important legal distinction between an offer and an invitation to treat and why it is so vital to a film company operating a website which sells merchandise.

There are many legislative requirements of websites in terms of the information they must display. The full extent of these depends on the range of services the website provides. Usually the film company would not simply sell DVDs. The company would want to supply information about its film catalogue, possibly offer cinema ticket purchase facilities and produce an online magazine (the legal terms for online magazine subscriptions are reviewed in Chapter 11). Certainly the company would want to gather information from its online consumers and it is highly likely that the website will utilise and display the intellectual property of the film company and third parties. For a website of reasonable sophistication, which provides a good range of content for film fans, there may well be at least nine separate pieces of legislation which must be complied with before the website can meet its full legal responsibilities. These include obligations under: the *E-Commerce Regulations 2002* (Chapter 4); *Data Protection Act 1998* (Chapter 7); the *Privacy and Electronic Communications Regulations 2002* (Chapter 6); the *Consumer Protection (Contracts Concluded by Means of Distance Communication)Regulations 2000* (Chapter 8); the *Unfair Contract Terms Act 1977* (Chapter 2); the *Unfair Terms in Consumer Contracts Regulations 1999*; the *Sale of Goods Act 1979*; the *Supply of Goods and Services Act 1982*; and the *Disability Discrimination Act 1995* (Chapter 14). In addition to these pieces of legislation there is also case law which interprets particular statutory provisions. There will be an ever-increasing bank of case law decisions turning on internet film distribution over the coming years as commercial use of the internet grows.

EXAMPLE CLAUSES FOR THE SUPPLY OF MERCHANDISE AND SERVICES ONLINE

The first point to note in the context of forming any contract with either consumers or potential business partners for any new media platform is the essential need to understand the technology. Only by such understanding can the film company fully appreciate its potential in terms of audience reach. The technology determines both the service that can be offered and also the precise legal control. Any legal contract designed to protect the film company needs to be platform specific. This is the only way that precision can be achieved in drafting, for example, intellectual property rights licences. The commercial basis of the platform also needs to be understood. Will the service be free, based on a subscription for a package, or perhaps on payment per single piece of content? The film company as content owner will want to limit the technological platform through which their content is delivered in each case so that they can maximise value. However, the licensee of the content will want whatever rights they acquire to be technology neutral so that their single licence covers all platforms, including emerging platforms.

The film company needs to know whether it intends to offer its content on a download-to-own basis, for example. What device does the company intend the content to be made available through? What will the exact functionality be? The timing of the service is important. Will the content be made available immediately or is there a delay in access? In short, its business objectives must be carefully thought through before any legal drafting takes place.

For present purposes we will examine the typical provisions to be included in the website terms and conditions for the online film company in its dealings with consumer purchasers.

As discussed earlier, the website terms and conditions must be brought to the attention of the user before the contract is concluded in order for those terms to be validly incorporated into the contract. Under English law the most effective way that this can be achieved is to require the visitor to click through the terms before being able to proceed further in the online ordering process. This is known as a 'click wrap' contract. The proper place for the display of the terms is at the point prior to the 'checkout' facility in the online basket on the website. This process is now likely to be familiar to all web users. The terms can also govern the sale if reasonable steps have been taken to bring them to the attention of the online consumer before the contract is entered into. It is unclear just how that might occur, but it is not safe to build a hyperlink on the website to the legal terms where that hyperlink appears at the bottom of a webpage requiring the visitor to scroll down to the page in order to even see the terms.[1]

There is some uncertainty in the context of mobile phone access to internet film websites. For example, if the film company wishes to market to its consumer base via their mobile telephones, there are clear rules it must follow. We consider in Chapter 6 how the film company must go about targeting and notifying those phone subscribers. If the web content produced by the film company contains an offer, for example, to buy a DVDs at discounted rates, the limitation in screen size of the mobile apparatus will almost certainly prevent the display on the page of full terms and conditions. Therefore the company

---

1   US case *Specht v Netscape Communications Corp*, 150 F Supp 2d 585 SDNY (3 July 2001).

might refer to the full terms in a prominent part of the webpage used by mobile phone visitors. Those terms might then be displayed on a website and the URL for that site listed in the mobile invitation. Whilst this is the only practical way to address the problem of notification of terms, one can see the difficulties it presents.

The opening paragraphs of the website terms and conditions should request that the visitor carefully reads the terms and that by clicking the 'I Accept' button, usually appearing at the bottom of the terms, the visitor agrees to be bound by the terms. The steps necessary for the visitor to conclude the contract must be set out as required by the E-Commerce Regulations 2002 (Chapter 4). It would be prudent for the film company to make clear that any delivery dates for merchandise stated in the website are estimates only and no liability will ensue for late delivery.

Every attempt must be made by the business to ensure that prices are correct, but usually the film company will insert a provision confirming that the order must be validated by it as part of the acceptance procedure. In this way, if the actual price of the article differs from that displayed on the website, the discrepancy can be picked up by the film company. It can then notify the purchaser of the correct price and the purchaser can then decide whether to cancel the order or proceed.

We noted at the beginning of this chapter that there is a very good reason why a website must be characterised as an invitation to treat rather than an offer for sale from a legal perspective. To reinforce this status it is important to insert a provision in the terms that the film company is entitled to refuse any order placed by its online consumer. If the order is accepted then the company should state that it will confirm acceptance by electronic means, usually to the e-mail address the consumer has indicated on registration or ordering. The film company should then specify a date by which the order will be fulfilled and perhaps a backstop date in the absence of a specified date.

Although it is more a commercial matter, the film company might want to consider the supply of alternative merchandise if the product ordered by the online consumer is not available. This will depend on the type of product to be supplied via the website and it is really a matter of how the company wishes to meet customer expectations. If it does want this flexibility then it should insert a clause in its terms to allow for supply of alternative products.

We now turn to the issue of the return of merchandise which has been ordered from a film website. We will consider in Chapter 8 the requirements of the Consumer Protection (Contracts Concluded by Means of Distance Communication) Regulations 2000.

It will be recalled that the online customer must be told their rights under those Regulations. The place to do this and to set out comprehensively the company's returns policy is in the legal terms on its website. The film company should state that the consumer has seven days in which to return any merchandise they have purchased and that this includes that the customer has simply changed their mind.[2] The customer must be instructed to notify the company in writing (which, of course, includes e-mail) within those seven days. The film company must then refund the customer as soon as possible. However, it is open to the film company to require the customer to be responsible for the costs of return post and packaging. If this is to be the case then it must be specified in the terms – it will not be considered to be implied by the courts. Clearly, the customer is under an obligation to keep the merchandise in good condition within the meantime and this must be pointed out to them.

It is useful at this juncture to remind the reader that this consumer right to return goods without question only applies to internet sales in the European Union and there are a number of exclusions. In the example website terms we are considering in this section we have assumed that the film website is supplying products such as DVDs and other physical merchandise. In each of these cases the online consumer has the benefit of the Distance Selling Regulations. However, if the film website also offers deals such as hotel accommodation and theatre ticket sales – in other words where the services are to be supplied on a particular date or specific period – then the Regulations will not apply. It would clearly be unfair for a consumer to accept such deals and then later cancel. It might not be possible for the film company to manage that cancellation or make the tickets or accommodation available to other members of its internet audience. In such cases the consumer does not have the right to a cancellation period of seven days. The other exception is the making available of online film for download against payment. In this instance, as we have seen, the film buyer cannot demand a refund or cancel the contract since the benefit has already been obtained.

It can be seen that a film website may be difficult to place properly in the legal environment which governs online sales. Some products available from the website allow the consumer return rights, others may not. It is important to

---

2   Consumer Protection (Distance Selling) DS Regulations 2000 (SI 2000/2334).

take advice from a new media lawyer with an understanding of internet issues to ensure that whatever terms the film company wishes to incorporate in its website are properly drafted. This advice should be taken early, as in reality it will impact on the overall online strategy to be adopted by the film company.

The other aspect in relation to returns brings into play long-established consumer legislation. The law implies certain warranties into consumer contracts whether they are for the sale of goods or for the provision of services. So, for example, the goods supplied must match their description[3] and they must be of satisfactory quality.[4] This includes their state and condition, fitness for purpose, appearance and finish, safety, durability and freedom from minor defects. In addition, the law implies a warranty that the goods are fit for a particular purpose if the seller knows that purpose except where the circumstances show that the buyer did not rely, or it was unreasonable for him or her to rely, on the skill or judgement of the seller.[5] All these matters are implied by law into internet sales of merchandise supplied by film companies to consumers. They cannot be excluded to any extent under the *Unfair Contract Terms Act 1977*. Even if the provisions were not included in the legal terms governing the website, the online consumer would benefit from their effect as the terms are implied by law. Clearly, it is desirable to address the implied warranties in the terms since, as we can see, a variety of other legal requirements needs to be incorporated.

However, where the internet film company is supplying goods to another business the position differs. The Unfair Contract Terms Act 1977 allows for the foregoing implied warranties to be limited, or indeed excluded, but this is subject to the test of reasonableness. It is not uncommon for film company websites to target both consumers and other businesses. This might depend upon the nature of the service being provided, but if this is the case careful thought needs to be given to the website terms. It will always depend on the actual nature of the film website and what it provides but as a rule two sets of legal terms would have to be drawn. Each would be accessed by a clearly worded guide notifying the website visitor which terms they must read (and then be forced through by way of the click-wrap contract explained above). Once again advice should be taken on this issue. There is a balance to be struck between proper legal compliance and populating the website with an abundance of legal terms.

---

3   Sale of Goods Act 1979 Section 13(1).
4   Sale of Goods Act 1979 Section 14(2).
5   Sale of Goods Act 1979 Section 14(3).

We have focused on the supply of merchandise via a website. The law, though, affords similar implied protection for consumers shopping online where the film company is supplying a service. This time the governing legislation is the *Supply of Goods and Services Act 1982*. The first requirement of this legislation is simple enough to grasp, though harder to test: it is that the supplier will carry out the services with reasonable care and skill.[6] Second, where the time for the services to be carried out is not specified in the contract but determined by a course of dealing between the parties, or left to be fixed in a manner agreed by the contract, the supplier will carry out the service within a reasonable time.[7] The same principle applies to the payment to be made for the services. Where the consideration for the services to be carried out is not specified in the contract but determined by a course of dealing, or to be agreed by the parties, the recipient of the services will pay a reasonable charge.[8] In view of the implied requirement, it is always better for the film company to fix the price of any services provided via the website.

One should note the constant reference to consideration as opposed to money. The law refers to a valid contract having 'consideration' as a vital constituent part of its ingredients. Without consideration there can be no contract. This is why some contracts contain a nominal sum of, say, £1 by way of price. This is clearly not the true value of the transaction but is inserted merely to satisfy the legal requirement that there be some consideration. Consideration can be money or money's worth. It might be that an online visitor can claim merchandise or the benefit of services on the website but the visitor must do something in return, not necessarily pay a sum of money. A contract can therefore be valid and satisfy the need for consideration in a number of forms.

Once again, it is apparent that the drafting of the website terms must be undertaken carefully. The position alters as between selling merchandise online to consumers and selling those goods to a business purchaser. The most effective treatment of the problem is for the online music business to have a satisfactory quality management and returns policy in place as a matter of commercial good sense. The use of legal terms, particularly those which seek to limit liability, offers further control over commercial exposure which, in the context of internet sales, is attractive. However, to ensure repeat internet traffic, first class service is always the best policy.

---

6   Supply of Goods and Services Act 1982 Section 13.
7   Supply of Goods and Services Act 1982 Section 14(1).
8   Supply of Goods and Services Act 1982 Section 14(1).

We now turn to the matter of data collection via the film website. The internet, of course, has made possible the capture of data to a degree hitherto not possible. It is that information which, in many ways, makes the medium so effective as a commercial tool. The data does not just include personal information in the form of a person's name and address. Software tracking devices afford internet vendors the ability to streamline the supply of goods and services to the visitor based on that visitor's previous buying behaviour. Recommendations as to other related purchases can be brought to their attention and thus greater sales achieved by this clever deployment of technology. Indeed, it is this ability to gather highly-targeted information about online consumers which is the principal attraction to the film company of making its content available over the internet. The internet market is revealing that people have interests in subjects and items which the mass audience might find curious. However, enough people may share the interest to make distribution of content to them commercially viable if the content owner can find them. Social networking websites such as MySpace, for example, are a hugely useful conduit for this targeted content.

As we will see in Chapter 7 in our review of the data protection regime there are, however, strict controls in the European Union as to the use of personally identifiable information. Those controls have huge significance for internet trade and the online film company must be cognisant of its legal obligations. The place where compliance with those data protection legal obligations must be achieved is the website terms.

CHAPTER 4

The Electronic Commerce (EC Directive) Regulations 2002

HOW FILM WEBSITES MUST OPERATE WITHIN THE LAW

There is now a plethora of film download websites, including Apple's iTunes and Amazon's Unbox service. The telecommunications giant AT&T has launched an internet television service that enables subscribers to view a selection of live and streamed TV channels on their PC over any wired or wireless broadband connection. These are, of course, trusted brands with high standards of customer care. However, with the growth of online film access, many other services will become available from a range of companies.

In 2002 – in response to a growing concern that consumers might become unwitting victims of virtual businesses which operate only online and who cannot be traced if they do not honour their obligations – the European Union introduced a set of regulations. These are designed to give consumers throughout the Union more confidence when buying goods or services over the internet. This protection only applies to consumers who visit commercial websites, but the requirements which the Regulations set down clearly dictate how any business website must operate.

In the United Kingdom the regulations are called the *Electronic Commerce (EC Directive) Regulations 2002 (FI2002No2013)*. They transpose the main requirements of the EU *E-Commerce Directive (2000/31/EC)* into UK law. Every film company website that offers merchandise or services must comply with the regulations, as must any website connected with the film industry where that website sells products or services. Failure to comply can lead to prosecution by the Trading Standards Department or Office of Fair Trading.

The E-Commerce Regulations (hereafter the Regulations) seek to encourage greater use of e-commerce by removing barriers across Europe and to enhance consumer confidence by clarifying the rights and obligations of business and consumers.

The Regulations also seek to promote the single market in Europe by ensuring the free movement of 'information society services' across the European Economic Area. That area includes the 27 member states of the European Union, together with Iceland, Norway and Liechstenstein. The term 'information society services' essentially means all commercial online services.

The Regulations have great relevance to the entertainment industry given that they have application to a film company if it advertises goods or services online. This includes:

- via the internet;

- on interactive television; and

- by mobile telephone.

Each of these routes to market lend themselves to the film industry and its need to secure the youth market.

The Regulations cover a number of aspects of electronic trade including provisions for the national law that will apply to online services. Second, the information a film company must give to its online consumers. These details include discounts and offers which might feature in an online advertising campaign and how to conclude contracts on its website.

The Regulations also set out limitations on a service providers' liability for any unlawful information it unwittingly carries or stores.

If a film company wishes to sell merchandise or render some service via its website it must meet its legal obligations enshrined in the Regulations. Non-compliance has consequences. For example, a filmgoer who purchased the latest DVD title from the website may cancel their order. They may seek a Court Order against the film company. They may also sue the company for breach of statutory duty if they can demonstrate that they have suffered loss because of the company's failure to comply with the Regulations.

If a film company operates a website which does not comply with the Regulations there are penalties which, in addition to the financial consequence, would also cause considerable damage to goodwill. Allied to the Regulations are the *Stop Now Orders (EC Directive) Regulations 2001*. These permit the Directors General of both Fair Trading and Trading Standards Departments in the UK to apply to the Court for a *Stop Now Order* if the film company's failure to comply with the Regulations 'harms the collective interest of consumers'. The Stop Now Order requires the film company to immediately cease operation of its website and take it offline. When one considers how vital the website might be to the film company and the perhaps numerous goods and services provided via the website, it can be seen that a Stop Now Order must be avoided. The website must remain offline until the corrective work has been completed. Given the significant financial loss that could ensue from the enforced shut down it is obviously important for film company website operators to ensure their websites comply with the Regulations in the first place.

The courts also have the power to order the publication of corrective statements with a view to eliminating the continuing effects of past infringements. Failure by a film company to comply with a Stop Now Order could result in its being held in contempt of court. The consequence of that might be a fine and/or imprisonment of its principal officers or directors.

A number of organisations can enforce the Regulations. Examples include Trading Standards departments, the Office of Fair Trading and the Independent Committee for the Supervision of Standards of Telephone Information Services (ICSTIS). It is important to appreciate that the risk of being identified as being in breach of the Regulations is high. Any consumer who visits the film website can report the film company to the appropriate body with a view to, for example, the Trading Standards Department then taking action against the film company.

The E-Commerce Regulations also impact on the question of whose law will apply to cross-border trade. Clearly, the distribution of film content either by dispatch of DVDs to another country or by online means is common. The Regulations liberalise the provision of online services in two key ways. First, they require a UK-established film company to comply with UK laws even if it is providing those services in another member state. In other words, the UK-established film company will have to comply with UK law even if it is providing its services to, for example, German recipients.

The Regulations also prevent the UK from restricting the provision of information society services from another member state in the EU. In essence, there is nothing to stop, for example, a French film company based in Paris from providing web-based music services available in the UK and targeted towards UK music-buying consumers.

However, these rules are subject to a number of qualifications and exclusions. We examine in Chapter 15 the importance of specifying which country's law will govern the online contract. The Regulations also include the freedom to choose the law which applies to an online contract and to specify certain contractual obligations with regard to consumer contracts made over the internet.

The Regulations do not, however, deal with the jurisdiction of the courts, that is, which court will hear a cross-border trading dispute between, for example, a film company based in the UK and an online games company based in Spain.

NEW INFORMATION REQUIREMENTS

The information requirements contained in the Regulations can be divided into three categories, which will be described below.

INFORMATION REQUIREMENTS

The film company must provide its consumer end users with full contract details of the organisation and details of any relevant trade organisations to which it belongs, for example the Producers Alliance for Cinema and Television (PACT). Details of any authorisation scheme relevant to its online business must also be made clear. If the business is making merchandise or services available via its website it will almost certainly fall within the VAT threshold. If so, its VAT Registration Number must be published on the website. There must be a clear indication of prices for the merchandise or service including any delivery or tax charges.

COMMERCIAL COMMUNICATIONS

The Regulations impose an obligation on the film company to provide its online customers with clear information concerning any electronic communications designed to promote (directly or indirectly) its merchandise, services or image. Examples of such electronic communications would include e-mails advertising its merchandise or services. In Chapter 12 we examine the broader requirements the film company must adhere to in terms of its online advertising. The E-Commerce Regulations build on those.

The film company must provide clear identification of the person on whose behalf the communication is sent. For example, the e-mail header might read 'Unsolicited Commercial Communication sent on behalf of Lecote Films Ltd'.

In addition, full details of any promotional offers advertised – for example, any discounts on merchandise, premium gifts, title competitions or games – must be provided. If the film company wishes to impose any qualifying conditions upon such special offers a full explanation of those conditions must be given.

ELECTRONIC CONTRACTS

As we have seen in Chapter 2 in relation to the formation of online contracts, the method by which a contract must be created over the internet is subject to a number of issues. The E-Commerce Regulations add to those more general stipulations. The essential information with which a film company must provide its online consumers is as follows.

The business must provide a description of the different technical steps to be taken to conclude a contract online. In other words, there must be clear guidance on the website as to how the contract to purchase a DVD, for example, is completed. We saw in our review of the film company's internet legal terms and conditions how those terms must be clicked through before the online consumer can proceed to the checkout section of the website. The Regulations say that it must be clear to the buyer at which point they will be legally bound. There must be no ambiguity. Further, the film company must provide confirmation of whether the contract will be filed by the company and whether it can be accessed. A clear identification of the technical means to enable its online customers to correct any inputting errors must be shown.

It may be that the film company operates across many jurisdictions or targets certain merchandise or services to particular countries. If this is the case an indication of the languages offered in which to conclude the contract must be displayed.

Remember, all these requirements embodied in the Regulations relating to electronic contracting apply to any film company which advertises or sells merchandise or services via the internet, mobile phone or interactive television.

So, let us consider in more detail the requirements of the E-Commerce Regulations.

The UK government recognises that technological constraints – for example the 160-character limit on a mobile phone text message – might mean that the film company may not be able to provide all the information required by the Regulations via the same means by which it transacts with its customer. This scenario becomes more common as the use of sophisticated 3G mobile phone services increases. There are more tie-ins between the film content owner and the mobile phone networks than ever before. Film trailer promotion on 3G phones is very popular. Commercial experience thus far obtained shows that phone subscribers are happy to view trailer content on their phones and the quality can be extremely high. However, to expect detailed legal terms to be available on the screen of the mobile phone is unrealistic. The government believes that the information requirements outlined above will be met if the information is accessible by other means. For example, if the online consumer purchases a film download via their mobile phone, the film company should be able to satisfy its requirements if it places the relevant information on its principal website.

Temporary interruptions to online services do arise from time to time. We saw in our review of the film company's website terms and conditions why it is important for the company to exclude liability for occasional transient disruption to its online service. The government also appreciates that temporary interruptions to the availability of information are essential – for example, for maintenance purposes – or unavoidable – for example, if the computer system crashes because of a virus. Such interruptions will not place the film company in breach of its legal obligations. That said, the need for a robust internet service is going to be of prime importance to the film company. Any unforeseen downtime or interruption to the online service is going to cause annoyance to the audience, which appears to be unforgiving when it comes to poor online functionality. Online audiences – which are hard to secure – can be easily lost as a result of downtime. This means that the relationship between the film company and its hosting company is key. It is why one will find penalties by way of service credits in typical hosting contracts. This issue is addressed in Chapter 10.

The point to appreciate is that the information requirements summarised above are in addition to other legal requirements. These include those under the *Consumer Protection (Contracts Concluded at a Distance) Regulations 2000*, which are discussed in Chapter 8. Among other things, these Regulations require the film company to provide a description of its merchandise or services, details of any guarantees offered and full details of its online customers' rights to cancel an order.

The website terms and conditions applicable to the film company's online contract must be made available in a way that allows the consumer to store and reproduce them. It is considered that this requirement will be satisfied if end users are able to save the terms and conditions onto their computer and subsequently print them out.

When the consumer places an online order with the film company it is necessary for the company to acknowledge receipt of the order without undue delay and by electronic means. It is important to remind the reader that this requirement does not apply to online transactions between two businesses, known as business-to-business transactions, if both parties agree to opt out of the Regulations. We examined in our review of online contracts generally in Chapter 2 the distinction between an offer and an invitation to treat and the dangers of sending an automatic electronic bounceback message to enquirers. It is therefore very important when adopting the form of electronic acknowledgement required by the Regulations that the text of that acknowledgement makes it clear that the acknowledgement is not a formal acceptance of the film company's online customer enquiry.

The E-Commerce Regulations also limit the liability of Internet Service Providers (ISPs) who unwittingly carry or store unlawful content provided by others in certain circumstances. If a film company wishes to strike a deal with one of the internet service providers for making film content available via the ISP, the ISP will almost certainly include a confirmatory clause in the agreement excluding their liability for certain content.

REFORM OF THE E-COMMERCE REGULATIONS

At the time of writing, the government is seeking views on whether the protection given to Internet Service Providers under the E-Commerce Regulations should be extended to cover providers of search engines and directories, providers of keyword advertising services and content aggregators. The government wants to assess whether the existing law is creating problems for providers of these services and, if so, whether an amendment to the Regulations is necessary. One problem which could arise, for example, is where a search engine links to film copyright material. The link potentially helps people to copy that material, as someone can infringe copyright by authorising another to act without the permission of the copyright owner. It is arguable that the link may itself be copyright infringement.

CHECKLIST

- Ensure that the film website contains full information as to the operator, including physical address and VAT Number.

- If sending electronic marketing messages to promote a title or merchandise, ensure it contains the appropriate e-mail header. Note also to whom unsolicited e-mails must be sent under the Privacy and Electronic Communications Regulations discussed in Chapter 6.

- Check that the legal terms and conditions on the film website are capable of being printed off by the online customer.

- Ensure that the visitor to the website is made fully aware of the steps necessary to conclude a contract via the film website.

- If using mobile phone text messaging to alert customers to marketing offers, ensure that a suitable and clear reference to the film website and the legal terms and conditions contained on that website is included.

CHAPTER 5

Protecting and Exploiting Intellectual Property Rights in Online Film and Television Content

COPYRIGHT AND THE INTERNET IN GENERAL

In many ways the principal threat to the filmmaker in the online world is not piracy, it is obscurity. The real challenge is getting your content to market.

In the new media world there are ever more platforms available when deciding where your content needs to be. From television on mobile phones and portable games players, videos for iPods, broadcast mobile television and WiFi TV, the plethora of delivery methods offers opportunity, but in each case the need to protect the intellectual property rights of the content owner is paramount.

A website operated by a film company will contain many elements, each of which will attract copyright protection. The website's text, graphics, advertisements, data and, of course, the film content. Thus, the suggestion that there is no such thing as copyright on the internet is clearly misplaced.

Copyright is a negative right. It is a right to restrain others from exploiting work without the owner's consent. In this country copyright is governed by the *Copyright, Designs and Patents Act 1988* which came into effect in 1989. Section 1(1) of that Act states that copyright may subsist in the following types of work:

(a) *original literary, dramatic, musical or artistic works,*

(b) *sound recordings, films, broadcasts or cable programmes, and*

(c) *the typographical arrangement of published editions.*

For a literary, dramatic, musical or artistic work to qualify for protection it must be original. This does not mean that, for example, the content needs to be novel or unique; it only has to originate from the writer – which means it must not be copied from any other work – and to embody a minimal degree of skill, judgement and labour.

Section 5A(1) states that sound recording copyright can subsist regardless of the medium on which the recording is made or the method by which the sounds are reproduced or produced.

For someone to gain the protection of the Act they must be a 'qualified person'. There are three ways in which to be so qualified. They must be British citizens or domiciled here or, if a company, be incorporated in the UK. Alternatively the work must be first published in the UK. Here lies a problem for the internet. It is not easy to be clear as to which country a work is said to have been first published. The third route is where the work is a broadcast or cable programme and is made or sent from the UK. Here again, problems can arise with the internet. However, it is rare for a work in the UK not to attract copyright protection because it has not met the above tests for qualification.

The 'author' is the person who creates the work, for example, the scriptwriter or screenwriter. The author is not always the 'owner' of the work. Ownership may be assigned to for example a film production company by the author.

The matter of how long a copyright work lasts is now dealt with in the Copyright and Related Rights Regulations 2003, which are considered in detail below.

THE CONVERGENCE OF MEDIA AND TECHNOLOGY

The rise in digital communications has changed the media landscape. Before we consider the laws that govern copyright in the digital age it is well to view that landscape fully, as it affords a helpful background as to why the law is so vital. The United Kingdom appears set to become the digital media capital. Growth in digital television and broadband has been rapid and the evidence is that consumers are accessing their media content via radio, television and the internet digitally.

A Report by OFCOM,[1] published in August 2004, serves as a useful barometer of where we are as a nation in terms of adoption of digital technology. According to the research 53 per cent of homes in the UK now receive digital television. The surge in viewers using digital TV has been driven by subscription

---

1   OFCOM Report entitled *The Communications Market 2004* – Overview dated 10 August 2004.

revenue, which has overtaken advertising revenue. Interactive services have proved to yield the highest demand. It is believed that by 2016 at least half of all programming will be accessed on-demand as technological advances make television content more accessible.

Digital radio has also achieved dramatic growth, with 2.5 per cent of UK households owning a DAB set. This is significant given the relative infancy of the format. The UK is the world leader in DAB digital radio.

In this book there is frequent reference to the convergence of media and technology and this is the issue which, in many instances, is causing the law difficulty. The convergence of traditional broadcasting and digital media is forcing the worlds of the television, the PC and the mobile phone together, creating significant challenges and opportunities for licensing content across these new media channels. Convergence is picked up by the OFCOM report, which highlights evidence of crossover in formats. Almost 29 per cent of all adults have listened to radio programmes using their television set. Half of all analogue radio stations can be heard through websites. The proliferation of television programmes delivered via the internet, digital radio delivered via television and several other permutations shows the huge shift that has occurred in recent years. Listening to radio via mobile phones has increased rapidly among 15–24 year olds. In 2004 one major radio group announced the launch of a 'hear it, buy it, burn it' service on its websites. Users can hear a song they like on the radio and then use the station's websites to download it to their MP3 player. The same service might just as easily govern a film download. A few years ago no one could have predicted that Nokia, the mobile phone manufacturer, would be the largest supplier of cameras. However, camera phones have proved hugely successful among consumers. Similarly, many observers find it interesting that iTunes, a technology company with no background in media content retail, is now the market leader. The company claims that it accounts for four out of every five digital music sales in the UK. In a very short space of time people are learning to use mobile devices to watch television, play games and listen to music. Laptops can be turned into televisions via services which stream content from cable or satellite boxes over the internet. Indeed, new laptops are really media centres. They have high definition screens enabling the user to watch film and television programmes with little diminution of quality. The mobile phone industry is starting to deliver television channels over its wireless networks. Services which are set for launch include Visual Radio, which lets the user listen to the radio, such as the soundtrack to a film, on their phones while viewing related information, such as film stills and production information. It is becoming clear that interactivity engages listeners and the advantages to the film company is that branding is enhanced, there is added visual appeal and they can deliver effective messaging to listeners.

There can be little doubt that the future is digital as there is a growing appetite for the delivery of all content, including entertainment, news and, of course, film in digital formats. In 2004 Universal Music UK, which has 26 per cent of the UK music sector and a portfolio of over 300,000 digitised tracks, launched a new service to enable the secure distribution of its music and video portfolio to mobile phones and handheld devices.

There is significant opportunity for the film industry to embrace all these platforms to increase market share but the plethora of apparatus creates legal complexities.

In tandem with this convergence of media and technology has come, of course, the illicit distribution of film via the internet. Until recently the only way a filmmaker could find an outlet for its titles was to convince an individual in one studio to take the film. However, the threat posed by internet film piracy to the established film industry is very real. Technological changes have always not only created problems for the film industry, but also ultimately opportunity and new windows. From the development of video cassettes capable of recording films off air from the television it has been a fact of modern commercial life. With the advent of the home computer and the internet, together with broadband availability, the problem has been made significantly worse. Today many PCs are equipped with a DVD 'burner' as standard. Software allows users to create their own film DVDs and a number of devices can also be used to play films that have been downloaded from the internet. The entertainment industry claims that this file trading has significantly harmed its revenues and that harm will only worsen as internet technology improves.

The issue is a global one and not restricted to the UK film industry. There exist a variety of 'peer-to-peer' internet services which will supply film for free in contravention of copyright. Peer-to-peer websites represent the 'superdistribution' of film. File sharing networks represent the greatest library of film in history. However, it seemed that those who sourced their film in this way did not have any sense that they were causing any hardship or that digital theft was wrong. Essentially the attitude was that if it is so easy and so widespread then it cannot be illegal. In addition, this attitude was fuelled by the fact that, from the early stirrings of e-commerce, much of the content available from the internet was free. Creating a culture of proper respect for creativity and effective protection of copyright is essential if the creative community is to be encouraged to make films available online. Improving communication and educational messages on copyright is therefore important for everyone in the digital value chain. A far higher proportion of online content is now paid for and is expected to be so. The music industry was the first to face the issue of illegal peer-to-peer file sharing. However, after some four years it seems that the music business is winning the battle. People are now prepared to pay 70p or so per track for a music download or enter into a subscription service. There is also a feeling that consumers were getting their own back on an industry that was perceived to be charging inflated prices for DVDs. So, in common with other content, in the early period of film being sourced online most of that availability was accessed for free. The ability to obtain film without payment is not the only attraction of the internet as a means of distribution. Many of those who download films do so because of the immediacy of access to film titles rather than acquiring, perhaps, a DVD, albeit purchased online.

In many ways the back catalogue distribution of titles via the internet is perhaps the best opportunity for a film company entering the online world. It already owns the content (subject to existing distribution deals which may have covered digital distribution). The internet, though, made it possible to acquire films from websites set up without the permission of the copyright holder, that is, the film company. Within a very short time these websites were attracting significant audiences because the catalogue of films they featured included current releases. There was a clear correlation between an alarming decrease in cinema attendances and an increase in peer-to-peer film file sharing. The internet had the obvious potential to become a zone for lawlessness where the normal rules of copyright did not apply.

This threat was increased with the arrival of compression programs, of which there are several types. The system developed to allow users to copy their DVDs to be downloadable either to play at home or for use on mobile players.

USER-GENERATED CONTENT

The latest threat to – although some may say opportunity for – the film and television industries is the growth of social networking websites. In late 2006 Universal Pictures in the United States began a legal action against the popular social networking website MySpace. The legal case followed a breakdown in negotiations between the two companies for a content licensing deal. In fact, Universal had similarly threatened legal action against another social networking website, YouTube, because that website specialises in video sharing.

However, Universal settled the case against YouTube for an equity share as part of Google's £841 million acquisition of the website. All such websites raise questions about the rights of copyright owners in relation to distribution of their content on the websites. In addition, these websites can attract significant advertising revenue (see Chapter 12) given their huge user base. They have become a major distribution channel for both video and music and hence a target for content owners, who are losing revenue as a result.

It is important to note that both YouTube and MySpace began life as user-generated websites rather than peer-to-peer websites. Peer-to-peer websites focus on distributing existing third party material as opposed to new, original material created by website members.

When Napster collapsed as a free peer-to-peer network following a successful copyright legal action by A&M Records, the only way for members of the network to obtain free music was to rely on unsigned bands who agreed to make their work available. User-generated websites thus began to develop, since their content is created and distributed almost exclusively by their members, as non-media professionals. User-generated websites also provide a powerful platform for independent content owners to promote their material to other users, who can recommend a video to other website users.

The distinction between peer-to-peer websites and user-generated websites has become blurred more recently as an increasing amount of non-user-generated content is uploaded. This is often the result of established content owners uploading their material in order to gain a greater audience. The problem is that a good deal of the content on these websites consists of copyrighted material being uploaded and circulated without permission. Both MySpace and YouTube show a catalogue of well-known advertisements, videos and clips from syndicated television programmes. The question is how such websites might be challenged in law in the UK.

In Chapter 4 we examined the Electronic Commerce (EC Directive) Regulations 2002. Regulation 17 of the same states that an intermediary service provider will not be liable for damages or criminal sanctions as a result of a transmission (such as the uploading of copyrighted material) provided that it:

a)   did not initiate the transmission;

b)   did not select the receiver of the transmission; and

c)   did not select or modify the information contained in the transmission.

Further, Regulation 19 provides that where a service provider stores information on its server it will not be liable for that information if:

a)   it has no actual knowledge of unlawful activity, or it is not aware of facts or circumstances from which an unlawful would have been apparent;

b)   upon obtaining such knowledge or awareness it acts expeditiously to remove or disable access to the information. The onus on establishing such awareness is on the party alleging that liability has arisen.

So, under the Regulations a service provider can be excluded from liability. However, the issue for determination will be whether it is reasonable for service providers to be able to rely on the exclusions while undoubtedly benefiting commercially from use of the copyright material. Next, is it unreasonable to impose on copyright owners an obligation to sift through the millions of items being transmitted daily so as to identify specific examples of copyright infringement? The legal position at the time of writing thus remains unclear.

The film industry subsequently began a fight back in an effort to win the hearts and minds of consumers, combined with a use of the law to frighten off would-be film file sharers.

A helpful starting point when reviewing whether merely providing the means to make illegal copies attracts legal liability is the 1984 'Sony' or Betamax' case. The United States Supreme Court had to decide whether or not the Betamax video machine was an illegal instrument of contributory copyright infringement. In *Sony v. Universal City Studios* 104 US 774 (1984) the Court had to determine the legality of the Betamax machine, which could both play pre-recorded films and videos legally and also could be used to record illegally. The court held that the machine was not illegal. The UK case of *CBS Songs v. Amstrad* (1988) RPC 567 came to a similar conclusion. The House of Lords held that there was no infringement of copyright in the marketing of a twin cassette deck that could clearly be used for infringing purposes, that is, of copying music cassettes without permission. It has therefore been apparent for some time that the provision of a service or equipment to facilitate copying, where that service or equipment has other legitimate uses, may not be an infringement or illegal.

The new laws considered below clearly provide the means to protect against unlawful film downloads but they do leave some anomalies. One can acquire an unwanted music DVD free with a weekend newspaper yet be subject to a fine if one downloads the same film from the internet. If someone spends a day listening to the radio and recording tracks for their MP3 player then that is to all practical purposes acceptable. However, if they download the same songs from the internet onto their iPod that is covered by the new Regulations.

Other commentators make the point that one consequence of the internet is that thousands of films might suddenly become available that would not physically fit on the shelves of those who acquire them. Should film companies have the right to extract royalties from titles that would not have seen the light of day but for the long reach of the internet?

For all the efforts of the industry, there is likely to be a degree to which they will always be helpless against the practical power of the internet. It is likely that studios will be forced to bring forward the release dates of their titles if they have appeared online before reaching the theatres. The internet is certainly seeing the collapsing of release windows so that theatre release, DVD release and broadcast in effect will become a single date. The fact is that as soon as something is recorded there is a real risk that it will find its way on to the internet.

More recently, the entertainment industries have turned their attention to the internet, and in particular the Internet Service Providers, telecommunications companies and software providers such as Verizon, Napster and Aimster.

THE DEVELOPMENT OF CASE LAW WHICH APPLIES TO ONLINE FILM

It is useful to review how the courts have approached the development of distributing media content, specifically music over the internet without the copyright holder's consent. The cases have centred on music distribution thus far because the music industry was the first to face the challenges the internet presents. In recent years a number of software programs became available which enabled the user to download music tracks via their PC either at home or at work. The music could be obtained free as it had been uploaded as a file by someone else and, through the power of the internet as a superdistribution channel, those works could be accessed anywhere in the world. The form of these software programs has altered and the manner in which music is accessed for free without the copyright holders consent is important in determining the precise legal basis for objection.

The largest market for music distribution and internet use is the United States and therefore it is of little surprise that the majority of the case law which has determined the issue is North American. Nonetheless, those cases serve as clear guidance as to how the UK has approached the problem in terms of both policy and legal argument.

In the United States the equivalent body to the UK's British Phonographic Industry (BPI) is the Recording Industry Association of America (RIAA). Faced with the explosion of internet file swappers downloading music from the internet for free the RIAA decided to take direct legal action. On behalf of the record companies as well as some artists the RIAA sought to sue Napster. The RIAA managed to obtain the subscriber and user details of those individuals who they considered were 'chronic' abusers of internet download services. In 2000 the organisation sought legal action in *RIAA v. Napster* (2000). File sharing software was made available on a central server which enabled users to see which other users had music in MP3 compressed form that they would like to acquire. This two-way link up to share music became known as peer-to-peer. Napster drew over 60 million users a day. The US District Court held that Napster's file swapping service was illegal. Napster had raised a variety of defences to the action by the RIAA. These included the argument rehearsed in previous eras and noted above, that the service had non-infringing as well as infringing uses. In addition, Napster argued that its service had the effect of boosting record sales and that the plaintiffs themselves were in the business of facilitating file-swapping, citing RIAA member Sony's manufacture of MP3 players. The court rejected all these arguments and granted an interim injunction against the file swapping service. Napster was found to have facilitated illegal copying by individual users and was ordered to pay significant damages. The company could not survive the damages award and ceased operation: it was declared bankrupt in 2002. The suspension of the Napster service drove users to other peer-to-peer websites.

The Napster case was followed by an action which represented a major victory for copyright holders in the US. In *RIAA v. Aimster* (2002) the record industry once again sought the assistance of the law in its fight against the unauthorised uploading and downloading of music. In 2001 Aimster had applied to the US District Court to have its service declared legal. The response from the RIAA, representing copyright holders, was to institute legal proceedings against Aimster alleging contributory and vicarious copyright infringements. The court accepted the RIAA arguments and determined that Aimster had clear knowledge of infringements taking place on its service. Further, Aimster had materially contributed to these infringements. In addition, Aimster could supervise the infringements if it so wanted and had benefited financially from these infringements. It was stated that Aimster was a service whose very *raison d'être* appeared to be the facilitation of and contribution to copyright infringement on a massive scale. Aimster was ordered to prevent users from uploading and downloading copyright works or cease operations if it could not do so and to employ technical measures to prevent copyright infringement.

The next case resulted in the RIAA suffering a setback. In *MGM Studios and Others v. Grokster & Streamcast Networks* (2003) the legal tide changed. In 2001 MGM had launched legal actions against KaZaA, Grokster and StreamCast Networks for contributory and vicarious copyright infringement. Given the need for urgent determination on the question, both sides to the dispute sought an expedited ruling on liability. The court decided in favour of StreamCast Networks and Grokster. The court was able to distinguish its decision from earlier cases on the following grounds:

1   the software had non-infringing uses;

2   the defendants had no actual knowledge of specific infringements and could not supervise infringements.

This latter point was important because, unlike the Napster system, the Grokster facility had no centralised system. File sharers on the internet could access each other's files without recourse to lists operated by the service provider.

Alongside the legal cases being brought, with some rapidity, against those organisations which operated music download facilities without the consent of the copyright holders, the RIAA went about taking legal action against serial users of such services. These, of course, included individuals in their homes who were taking advantage of the ability to obtain music for free via the internet. With this tactic the RIAA was seeking to make examples of those people and to send a message out to other individuals tempted to do the same thing. This approach brought to the public attention the case of Brianna Lahara, then aged 12 years, who had a love of television theme music, the successful artist Christina Aguilera and the nursery song *If You're Happy and You Know It*. Her mother agreed to pay $2,000 in compensation. The RIAA issued a statement announcing the settlement and quoting the little girl as saying 'I am sorry for what I have done. I love music and don't want to hurt the artists I love'.

This tactic of making examples of individuals who download music illegally was to be followed in the UK two years later. This approach was considered by some to be a high risk public relations strategy. Many questioned the wisdom of multi-million pound companies suing individuals of modest means. However, the strategy of a sustained public relations campaign aimed at dissuading individuals from downloading music illegally and legal proceedings appears to have been highly effective.

In this country the courts have also been asked to decide on legality of facilitating copyright infringement. In *Sony Music Entertainment (UK) Ltd v. Easyinternetcafe Ltd* (2003) the High Court held that Easyinternetcafes were guilty of copyright infringement by allowing customers to download music without permission and to burn CD copies of these at Easyinternet's chain of cafes.

In June 2005 the United States Supreme Court tried to balance the competing demands of copyright owners and technology developers in a ruling which serves as the best guide to how the US courts approach the issue. In *MGM v. Grokster* (2005) the court held that the distributors of peer-to-peer software could be liable for infringements committed with their software. The court reached the conclusion by the use of the concept of active inducement from the US Patent Act. At the same time, the court affirmed that the distributor of a product used to infringe will not incur liability by virtue of the act of distribution so long as the product is capable of a substantial non-infringing use. On the face of it the latest chapter in the Grokster saga appears to be a music industry victory. The Supreme Court reversed the United States Federal Court of Appeals Ninth Circuit decision which had found that Grokster had no case to answer with regard to the use of its file sharing software to transfer illegally copied files. The Plaintiffs had argued what is known as 'active inducement'. Active inducement concentrates on the defendant's conduct rather than their technology. The court found that one who distributes a device with the object of promoting its use to infringe copyright, as shown by clear expression or other affirmative steps taken to foster infringement, is liable for the resulting acts of infringement by third parties.

It is considered that the decision has powered the digital future of legitimate US online businesses including file sharing networks by making those who promote theft accountable. The concern on the part of technology innovators is that the case has created a new era of uncertainty for software innovation.

It is clear that a distributors mere knowledge of infringing potential or actual infringement would not be enough to subject the distributor to liability.

It is possible in light of these various cases to assess some of the tests which courts might consider when reviewing software technology which has both infringing and non-infringing uses.

First, are there substantial non-infringing uses and the defendant has the opportunity to prove this. This was the issue in the Sony Betamax, *MGM v. Grokster*, and *RIAA v. Aimster* cases. Second, does the software provider have clear knowledge of infringing uses? Wilful blindness is no defence as in the decision in the *RIAA v. Aimster*, *Grokster* and *Napster* cases. Third, is the provider able to supervise infringement if it so wanted? This issue was considered in the Easyinternet case. Fourth, has the software provider materially contributed to infringements? For example, does it provide any assistance to those individuals who infringe? Finally, does the software provider financially benefit from infringing uses even where the provider is not infringing itself?

There are interesting commercial dynamics behind the recent cases on the question of internet film downloads. These surround the ownership consolidation in the music and entertainment industries. For example, AOL Time Warner is a company with businesses on both sides of the divide. It owns AOL and two major cable companies, together with a major record label, film and television interests. Sony owns a major record label in Sony Music, but is also a major producer of music equipment, including recording equipment and MP3 players.

Then there is the issue as to why the record industry appeared not to plan for the advent of the internet. Some industry commentators assert that the major record labels missed the boat when it came to the worldwide web. Apple still maintains a lead with legitimate downloads of music through its iTunes service. This is in contrast to the film industry's comprehensive commercial reaction to the threat of the VHS machine. The record industry failed to implement a business plan to deal with both the threat and opportunities presented by the internet. It is now for the film industry to once again act as it did when faced with the VHS machine.

At the time of writing the evidence is that fear of prosecution is deterring people from downloading music illegally. The uptake of legal download services increased by around 75 per cent in the year 2004 to 2005. Many people who had previously downloaded music from unauthorised websites claimed they would download less often in the future.

The platform for the UK film industry to fight back using the law is the Copyright and Related Rights Regulations 2003, considered below. The Regulations enable the protection of legal interests and the policing and enforcement of rights in film copyright across Europe. It is this framework which has assisted the British Phonographic Industry in its efforts to combat piracy in high-profile and effective legal actions. In essence, the UK music industry has conducted a well-constructed media campaign supported by legal action to change the mindset of music consumers. This strategy is also being deployed by the film industry.

It has been an impressive effort. For the past few years the music industry has been predicting the death of the singles market because of illegal downloading. However, figures produced in 2005 by the British Phonographic Industry (BPI) showed that single sales were increasing. In fact, the figures do not offer the complete picture as they often still refer to sales of what are known as 'physical' singles. If legal downloads are included, sales of singles have soared. Far from killing the industry, downloads have given it a new lease of life. In the year 2004–2005 the number of tracks sold over the internet reached 10 million. The combination of old and new has breathed new life into the pop single, sales of which had been dwindling for a decade. Sales of digital downloads in the UK increased 744 per cent in the second quarter of 2004. According to the BPI, 5,562,638 digital downloads were sold in the second quarter of 2005, almost twice the level of 2004.

The effort made by the British record industry has been matched on an international level in a coordinated global assault on internet piracy. In 2005 The International Federation of the Phonographic Industry (IFPI) filed a new wave of criminal and civil legal actions against significant uploaders who place hundreds of copyrighted songs on the internet file sharing networks without the permission of the copyright owners. The action targeted 963 individuals in 11 countries including Austria, Denmark, France, Italy, Germany, the Netherlands, Finland, Ireland, Iceland, Japan and the United Kingdom. The IFPI claimed its approach had worked, citing Germany as an example, where the number of files downloaded fell sharply in 2004, down 35 per cent to 382 million files compared to 602 million the previous year.

The experience of the music industry serves as a valuable lesson for the film business. In a sense the message of internet distribution is 'if it doesn't kill you it makes you stronger'. There are undoubtedly new audiences to be secured via the internet and new relationships to be negotiated with the new gatekeepers to market such as the telecommunications companies.

THE COPYRIGHT AND RELATED RIGHTS REGULATIONS 2003

BACKGROUND

How then has the law had to adapt to meet this new era? As we have noted, in English law copyright is governed by the *Copyright, Designs and Patents Act 1988*. This legislation brought a good deal of previous law in the sphere of copyright together under one statute, but in the almost 20 years since its introduction the world of media technology has changed completely. It was clear that new provisions would have to be drafted to properly transpose the fundamental principles contained in the 1988 Act to address the digital age. The result of a lengthy and detailed consultation process is the *Copyright and Related Rights Regulations 2003* which came into effect in England and Wales on 31 October 2003.

In essence, the new Regulations attempt to clarify the rights of those who own copyright in literary, dramatic, musical or artistic work, or in a sound recording or broadcast, when the media by which those works can be distributed are multifarious. Copyright and related rights give the filmmaker or other rightholder – for example, the studio – the exclusive right to undertake or authorise reproduction – that is, the copying – of their film content, in addition to the right to distribute copies to the public, and communicate their film to the public, for example, by showing or playing the film in public. Finally, the filmmaker or other rightholder also has the right to broadcast the film, including making it available in a cable programme service, or making an adaptation of the film. Infringement occurs when any of the above acts are carried out or authorised by a party without the consent or licence of the copyright owner or rightholder.

PROVISIONS RELATING TO BROADCASTS

The Regulations amend the definition of a broadcast, and Section 4 states that:

> 'broadcast' means an electronic transmission of visual images, sounds or other information which is transmitted for simultaneous reception by members of the public and is capable of being lawfully received by them,

or is transmitted at a time determined solely by the person making the transmission for presentation to members of the public.

Broadcasting means wired or wireless. It is important to note that this definition does not include use of the internet per se unless the transmission via the internet accompanies another transmission by, for example, television.

The section says:

Excepted from the definition of 'broadcast' is any internet transmission unless it is

(a)   a transmission taking place simultaneously on the internet and by other means,

(b)   a concurrent transmission of a live event, or

(c)   a transmission of recorded moving images or sounds forming part of a programme service offered by the person responsible for making the transmission, being a service in which programmes are transmitted at scheduled times determined by that person.

So one can see that a theatre performace, for example, which is transmitted live on television and which is simulcast via the internet would be included in the definition of broadcast as far as the internet characterisation of the programme is concerned.

The Regulations go on to clarify which acts are restricted by copyright in Section 6 headed

Infringement by communication to the public;

(1)   The communication to the public of the work is an act restricted by the copyright in

(a)   a literary, dramatic, musical or artistic work,

(b)   a sound recording or film, or

(c)   a broadcast.

(2)   References ... to communication to the public are to communication to the public by electronic transmission, and in relation to a work include

(a)   the broadcasting of the work;

> *(b) the making available to the public of the work by electronic transmission in such a way that members of the public may access it from a place and at a time individually chosen by them.'*

It appears from this section that a communication to the public is restricted, whether it be by broadcast – for example, television and radio – or by electronic transmission whereby the public can access it where and when they like, such as the internet or by the use of 'on demand' services.

THE MAKING AVAILABLE RIGHT

One significant revision of the 1988 Act is the introduction of the Making Available Right for performers. Section 182CA states that consent is required for making available to the public.

> *A performer's rights are infringed by a person who, without his consent, makes available to the public a recording of the whole or any substantial part of a qualifying performance by electronic transmission in such a way that members of the public may access the recording from a place and at a time individually chosen by them.*
>
> *The right of a performer under this section to authorise or prohibit the making available to the public of a recording is referred to ... as the 'making available right'.*

As with all copyright rules that came before the new Regulations, there are certain actions which, by their nature, do not constitute a significant breach of copyright and are as such permissible under the law.

Making Temporary Copies

Section 8 provides that 'the copyright ... in a ... film work ... is not infringed by the making of a temporary copy which is transient or incidental, which is an integral and essential part of a technological process and the sole purpose of which is to enable

> *(a) a transmission of the work in a network between third parties by an intermediary; or*
>
> *(b) a lawful use of the work;*
>
> *and which has no independent economic significance'.*

Research and Private Study

The Regulations also alter the definition of so-called 'fair dealing' in copyright work. The new provision is clear enough from the following reproduction of its phrasing. Section 9 now states that;

> *Fair dealing with a ... film ... work for the purpose of research for a non commercial purpose does not infringe any copyright in the work provided that it is accompanied by a sufficient acknowledgement.*

The section goes on to say that no acknowledgment of the kind detailed above is required where this would be impossible for reasons of practicality or otherwise.

Further, fair dealing 'with a ... film ... work for the purposes of private study does not infringe any copyright in the work'.

A new element to the extent of fair dealing is the clear direction in relation to computer programs. Such programs might, of cours,e be related to the online distribution of film. The new paragraph says:

> *It is not fair dealing to observe, study or test the functioning of a computer program in order to determine the ideas and principles which underlie any element of the program.'*

Criticism, Review and News Reporting

There are also changes to the position on fair dealing in the context of criticism, review and news reporting of, for example, a film release.

Section 10 says that:

> *Fair dealing with a performance or recording for the purpose of criticism or review, of that or another performance or recording, or of a work, does not infringe any of the rights ... provided that the performance or recording has been made available to the public.*

Film promotion features such methods as a trailer to accompany the release. In relation to the exceptions to copyright infringement, the Regulations make clear that certain things can be done with copyright film works for the purposes of instruction or examination. The new law says that:

> *Copyright in a sound recording, film or broadcast is not infringed by its being copied by making a film or film soundtrack in the course of instruction, or of preparation for instruction, in the making of films or film soundtracks, provided the copying*

(a)   is done by a person giving or receiving instruction, and

(b)   is accompanied by a sufficient acknowledgement

and provided the instruction is for a non commercial purpose.

There are other circumstances where certain copying is permitted but these do not require elaboration in this book. They include provisions relating to recordings by educational establishments of broadcasts, provisions relating to copying by librarians and the observing, studying and testing of computer programs. The latter covers the situation where the study or testing of the functionality of the program is undertaken in order to determine the ideas and principles which underlie any element of the program. If this is done while, for example, running the program – which one is entitled to do – then the copying is permitted.

Provisions Relating to Recording for the Purposes of Time Shifting

Where a copy which would otherwise be an infringing copy is made ... but which is subsequently dealt with

a)   it shall be treated as an infringing copy for the purposes of that dealing; and

b)   if that dealing infringes copyright, it shall be treated as an infringing copy for all subsequent purposes.

'Dealt with' means sold or let for hire, offered or exposed for sale or hire or communicated to the public.

It is important to distinguish pure domestic time shifting and the Regulations state:

(1) The making in domestic premises for private and domestic use of a recording of a broadcast solely for the purpose of enabling it to be viewed or listened to at a more convenient time does not infringe any right ..in relation to a performance or recording included in the broadcast.

However the Regulations make clear:

(3)   Where a recording which would otherwise be an illicit recording is made in accordance with this paragraph but is subsequently dealt with

a)   it shall be treated as an illicit recording for the purposes of that dealing; and

b)   *if that dealing infringes any right … it shall be treated as an illicit recording for all subsequent purposes.*

CIRCUMVENTING TECHNICAL MEASURES

It is new technologies which have created the problem of internet piracy: it is new technologies which in many ways are the best form of resistance. The obvious answer is for film companies to install technology in their titles which would monitor when and where they were used. This would prevent film content being viewed to unless the copyright was identified as legitimate. Huge resources have been put into anti-piracy devices, including watermarking and other methods to track the copying of film to control it and ensure proper payment. Other systems seek to create permanent and temporary passwords on computer files which permit only one copy of a file to be made and played on a legitimate player. Making one copy destroys one of the passwords: if an attempt is made to copy once more, the copy will not play because the player can only find one of the required two passwords. There are many such systems at the time of writing, but they probably only make it more difficult for film pirates rather than solve the problem fully. A useful example is the difficulties presented by installing copyright protection in DVDs. These contain deliberate errors which make it harder to copy the film. However, these errors mean that many legitimate DVDs cannot be used in the DVD drives of some computers. Nonetheless, the role of digital rights management in acquiring and delivering content for the mobile market for example is vital.

Digital Rights Management covers a range of issues. It includes encryption of content, licensing and authentication of identity of users. There are differing forms of Digital Rights Management including the forensic watermarking described above. Another is geo-filtering, the technical process which controls where the user is. For example, a credit card merchant can tell where the user is located. Such geo-filtering makes territorial restrictions on the use of content safe. In addition, Internet Service Providers (ISPs) can tell where a user is and prevent access as appropriate. There are also time limitations, such as how many burns the user can achieve before the time expires. Copy protection technology controls how many copies may be made of the content. Each of these methods of copyright control may be termed Digital Rights Management.

As an aside, there are some interesting legal issues at play with the use of Digital Rights Management technologies. For example, if you have purchased this book you may read it as many times as you like and wherever you like. However, Digital Rights Management on a film download restricts such unfettered use.

Although it is therefore very difficult to develop technology to prevent infringement, by virtue of the Copyright and Related Rights Regulations 2003 the European Union and the United Kingdom insist on strict legal protections for technology-driven devices. In essence the requirement, common throughout the EU, is that member states provide adequate legal protection against the circumvention of any effective technological measures which the person concerned carries out in the knowledge, or with reasonable grounds to know, that he or she is pursuing that objective.

The Definition of Technological Measures

Before considering how attempts to get around technical processes designed to stop copyright infringement are unlawful, it is worth setting out how the Regulations define 'technological measures'. Section 296ZF says that technological measures are any technology, device or component which is designed, in the normal course of its operation, to protect a copyright work other than a computer program. They are 'effective' if the use of the work is controlled by the copyright owner through:

> a)   an access control or protection process such as encryption, scrambling or other transformation of the work; or
>
> c)   a copy control mechanism
>
> which achieves the intended protection.

It can be seen that the definition would include the various forms of Digital Rights Management outlined above.

When reference is made to protecting film works, this is defined to mean the prevention or restriction of acts that are not authorised by the copyright owner and are restricted by copyright. The use of the film work does not extend to any use of the work that is outside the scope of the acts restricted by copyright.

Circumvention of Technological Measures

Technical developments allow film copyright holders to make use of technological measures designed to prevent or restrict acts not authorised by them. The threat is that illegal activities might be carried out in order to enable or facilitate the circumvention of technical protection provided by these measures.

Section 296ZA of the Regulations applies where:

(a) *effective technological measures have been applied to a copyright work other than a computer program; and*

(b) *a person (B) does anything which circumvents those measures knowing, or with reasonable grounds to know, that he is pursuing that objective.*

The following people have legal rights against B:

(a) *a person*

  (i)   *issuing to the public copies of, or*

  (ii) *communicating to the public,*

  the work to which effective technological measures have been applied; and

(b) *the copyright owner or his exclusive licensee, if he is not the person specified in paragraph (a).*

Devices and Services Designed to Circumvent Technological Measures

Under Section 296ZB 'Devices and services designed to circumvent technological measures':

(1) *A person commits an offence if he*

  (a) *manufactures for sale or hire, or*

  (b) *imports otherwise than for his private and domestic use, or*

  (c) *in the course of a business*

    (i)   *sells or lets for hire, or*

    (ii)   *offers or exposes for sale or hire, or*

    (iii) *advertises for sale or hire, or*

    (iv)   *possesses, or*

    (v)   *distributes, or*

  (c) *distributes otherwise than in the course of a business to such an extent as to affect prejudicially the copyright owner,*

  any device, product or component which is primarily designed, produced, or adapted for the purpose of enabling or facilitating the circumvention of effective technological measures.

(2) *A person commits an offence if he provides, promotes, advertises or markets*

   (a) *in the course of a business, or*

   (b) *otherwise than in the course of a business to such an extent as to affect prejudicially the copyright owner,*

a service the purpose of which is to enable or facilitate the circumvention of effective technological measures.

Under Section (4) a person guilty of an offence under subsections (1) or (2) above is liable:

   (a) *on summary conviction, to imprisonment for a term not exceeding three months, or to a fine not exceeding the statutory minimum, or both;*

   (b) *on conviction on indictment to a fine or imprisonment for a term not exceeding two years, or both.*

(5) *It is a defence to any prosecution for an offence under this section for the defendant to prove that he did not know, and had no reasonable grounds for believing, that*

   (a) *the device, product or component; or*

   (b) *the service,*

enabled or facilitated the circumvention of effective technological measures.

Who Can Sue Those who Use Devices and Services Designed to Circumvent Technological Measures?

The question arises as to who actually has the right to take legal action against someone who attempts to get around the copyright technical safeguards applied to film content. Section 296ZD of the Regulations provides the answer. If effective technological measures have been applied to a film copyright work and someone manufactures, imports, distributes, sells or advertises or simply has in his or her possession a device or provides services which are promoted advertised or marketed for the purpose of the circumvention, or have only a limited commercially significant purpose other than to circumvent, or are primarily designed to enable circumvention then the following people will have legal rights against that person:

- a person issuing to the public copies of or communicating to the public the film work to which effective technological measures have been applied;

- the actual copyright owner or his exclusive licensee;

- the owner or exclusive licensee of any intellectual property right in the effective technological measures applied to the film work.

Each of these people can take legal action against the infringer demanding delivery up or seizure of the products in question.

Electronic Rights Management Information

The Regulations also provide legal protection in the sphere of electronic rights management. Rights Management Information is defined as any information provided by the copyright owner or the holder of any right under copyright, which identifies the work, the author, the copyright owner or the holder of any intellectual property rights, or information about the terms and conditions of use of the work, and any numbers or codes that represent such information.

Section 296ZG says that it is unlawful where a person knowingly and without authority, removes or alters electronic rights management information associated with a copy of a copyright work. It is also unlawful if a person knows he or she is inducing, enabling, facilitating or concealing an infringement of copyright.

In addition, section 296ZG (2) covers someone who knowingly and without authority distributes, imports for distribution or communicates to the public, copies of a copyright work from which electronic rights management information has been removed or altered. If that person knows or has reason to believe, that by so doing he or she is inducing, enabling, facilitating or concealing an infringement of copyright.

Criminal Offences

The Regulations introduce new criminal offences in circumstances where there has been infringement as follows:

A person who infringes copyright in a work by communicating the work to the public

a)   *in the course of a business, or*

b)   *otherwise than in the course of a business to such an extent as to affect prejudicially the owner of the copyright, commits an*

*offence if he knows or has reason to believe that, by doing so, he is
infringing copyright in that work.*

The Regulations state that a person guilty of an offence above is liable:

a)   *on summary conviction to imprisonment for a term not exceeding
three months or a fine not exceeding the statutory maximum, or
both;*

b)   *on conviction on indictment to a fine or imprisonment for a term
not exceeding two years, or both.*

A person who infringes a content owner's making available right

a)   *in the course of a business, or*

b)   *otherwise than in the course of a business to such an extent as to affect
prejudicially the owner of the making available right,*

*commits an offence if he knows or has reason to believe that, by doing so, he is
infringing the making available right in the recording.*

A person guilty of an offence above is liable:

a)   *on summary conviction to imprisonment for a term not exceeding three
months or a fine not exceeding the statutory maximum, or both;*

b)   *on conviction on indictment to a fine or imprisonment for a term not
exceeding two years, or both.*

The Regulations also seek to enforce legal remedies against service providers in
the context of copyright infringement.

The High Court has power to grant an injunction against a service provider,
where the service provider has actual knowledge of another person using their
service to infringe copyright. The court clearly will have to determine whether
a service provider has actual knowledge and it will take into account all matters
which, in the particular circumstances, appear to it to be relevant. Amongst
other things, the court shall have regard to:

a.   *whether a service provider has received a notice which includes
the full name and address of the sender of the notice and details
of the infringement in question. It is important to note that the
definition of service provider in the context of the Copyright
and Related Rights Regulations have the same meaning given
to it by regulation 2 of the Electronic Commerce (EC Directive)
Regulations 2002. (considered in Chapter 4).*

The High Court also has power to grant an injunction against a service provider where that service provider has actual knowledge of another person using their service to infringe a performer's property right. Once again, in determining whether a service provider has actual knowledge the court will apply the same test detailed above.

The Regulations provide certain rights to those who hold merely a non-exclusive license in relation to copyrighted works.

A non-exclusive licensee may bring an action for infringement of copyright if:

a) *the infringing act was directly connected to a prior licensed act of the licensee, and the licence itself*

   i) *is in writing and is signed by or on behalf of the copyright owner; and*

   ii) *expressly grants the non-exclusive licensee a right of action under the section in the Regulations.*

The non-exclusive licensee has the same rights and remedies as the actual copyright owner would have had if it was he who had brought the legal action. The copyright owner still has his or her own rights if he or she chooses to use them.

Duration of Copyright in Sound Recordings

The Regulations amend the Copyright, Designs and Patents Act 1988 on the matter of how long copyright lasts in a work.

Section 29 of the Regulations state that copyright expires:

   i. *at the end of the period of 50 years from the end of the calendar year in which the recording is made, or*

   ii. *if during that period the recording is published, 50 years from the end of the calendar year in which it is first published, or*

   iii. *if during that period the recording is not published but is made available to the public by being played in public or communicated to the public, 50 years from the end of the calendar year in which it is first so made available.*

But in determining whether a sound recording has been published, played in public or communicated to the public, no account shall be taken of any unauthorised act.

CREATIVE COMMONS

One interesting recent development is the availability of what is known as Creative Commons. Creative Commons began in the United States in 2001 with the aim of establishing a fair middle way between the extremes of copyright control and the unsolicited exploitation of intellectual property. The creator-led scheme encourages writers, musicians and artists to give up some of their rights – for example, the right to distribute work or to control derivative works – to the 'commons' of the internet. This is achieved via a system of off-the-peg licences which are machine readable. Its primary tool is the use of a range of copyright licences which are freely available for public use. The licences allow creators to fine tune control over their work to enable as wide a distribution as possible. In essence the copyright holder is able to set out terms of use when they create their work. They might, for example, state that they are content for others to use their work for any reason as long as it is not for commercial purposes. Alternatively, they might permit use of commercial purposes. In this way, ideas can be protected but the author is able to encourage some other uses of their work. It is in effect a label saying 'Some rights reserved' as opposed to the usual copyright protection of 'All rights reserved'. The artist keeps his or her copyright but allows people to copy and distribute their work provided they are given credit as writers. The idea is to give the public access to, for example, archive footage from the different archives so they can use it to create new things, for example, to make their own video.

The Creative Commons concept has just been introduced in the United Kingdom following careful work by a legal team at Oxford University's 'Programme in Comparative Media Law and Policy'. Channel 4 in the UK is using the Creative Commons licences scheme for a music video service which it calls PixnMix. The concept behind Creative Commons is to allow for content to be introduced into the online environment so that it can be shared fully but also protected.

In the United Kingdom there are two different licences. One for England and Wales and one for Scotland to reflect the differing legal jurisdictions.

Creative Commons is at an early stage of life but it has already had some impact on the music industry, with some artists being persuaded to release their content under a Creative Commons licence.

There are some in the entertainment industry who express concern over Creative Commons, fearing that it undermines traditional copyright protection. They believe that content owners may unwittingly give away their rights irrevocably. In addition it could result in content owners who sign Creative Commons licences being discounted by a film company hostile to the concept. At the time of completion of this book it is not possible to assess the likely impact Creative Commons will have on film distribution in the digital era.

CREATIVE COMMONS SPECIMEN LICENCE

CREATIVE COMMONS

LEGAL CODE
Attribution – NoDerivs 2.0 England and Wales
CREATIVE COMMONS CORPORATION IS NOT A LAW FIRM AND DOES NOT PROVIDE LEGAL SERVICES, DISTRIBUTION OF THIS LICENCE DOES NOT CEATE AN ATTORNEY-CLIENT RELATIONSHIP. CREATIVE COMMONS PROVIDES THIS INFORMATION ON AN 'AS-IS' BASIS. CREATIVE COMMONS MAKES NO WARRANTIES REGARDING THE INFORMATION PROVIDED, AND DISCLAIMS LIABILITY FOR DAMAGES RESULTING FROM ITS USE.
Licence THE WORK (AS DEFINED BELOW) IS PROVIDED UNDER THE TERMS OF THIS CREATIVE COMMONS PUBLIC LICENCE ("CCPL" OR "LICENCE"). THE WORK IS PROTECTED BY COPYRIGHT AND/OR OTHER APPLICABLE LAW. ANY USE OF THE WORK OTHER THAN AS AUTHORISED UNDER THIS LICENCE OR COPYRIGHT LAW OS PROHIBITED. BY EXERCISING ANY RIGHTS TO THE WORK PROVIDED HERE, YOU ACCEPT AND AGREE TO BE BOUND BY THE TERMS OF THIS LICENCE. THE LICENSOR GRANTS YOU THE RIGHTS CONTAINED HERE IN CONSIDERATION OF YOUR ACCEPTANCE OF SUCH TERMS AND CONDITIONS.

This Creative Commons England and Wales Public Licence enables You (all capitalised terms defined below) to view, edit, modify, translate and distribute Works worldwide, under the terms of this licence, provided that You credit the Original Author.

'The Licensor' (one or more legally recognised persons or entities offering the Work under the terms and conditions of this Licence.)

and

'You'

agree as follows:

1. **Definitions**

    a. **'Attribution'** means acknowledging all the parties who have contributed to and have rights in the Work or Collective Work under this Licence.

    b. **'Collective Work'** means the Work in its entirety in unmodified form along with a number of other separate and independent works, assembled into collective whole.

    c. **'Derivative Work'** means any work created by the editing, modification, adaptation or translation of the Work in any media (however a work that constitutes a Collective Work will not be considered a Derivative Work for the purposes of this Licence). For the avoidance of doubt, where the Work is a musical composition or sound recording, the synchronisation of the Work in timed-relation with a moving image ('synching') will be considered a Derivative Work for the purpose of this Licence.

    d. **'Licence'** means this Creative Commons England and Wales Public Licence agreement.

    e. **'Original Author'** means the individual (or entity) who created the Work.

    f. **'Work'** means the work protected by copyright which is offered under the terms of this Licence.

    g. For the purpose of this Licence, when not inconsistent with the contracts, words in the singular number include the plural number.

2.   Licence Terms

2.1   The Licensor hereby grants to You a worldwide, royalty-free, non-exclusive, Licence for use and for the duration of copyright in the Work.

You may:

- copy the Work;

- incorporate the Work into one or more Collective Work; and

- publish, distribute, archive, perform or otherwise disseminate the Work or the Work as incorporated in any Collective Work, to the public in any material form in any media whether now known or hereafter created.

HOWEVER,

You must not:

- impose any terms on the use to be made of the Work or the Work as incorporated in a Collective Work that alter or restrict the terms of this Licence or any rights granted under it or has the effect or intent of restricting the ability to exercise those rights;

- impose any digital rights management technology on the Work or the Work as incorporated in a Collective Work that alters or restricts the terms of this Licence or any rights granted under it or has the effect or intent of restricting the ability to exercise those rights;

- make any Derivative Works;

- sublicence the Work;

- subject the Work to any derogatory treatment as defined in the Copyright, designs and Patents Act 1988.

FINALLY,

You must:

- make reference to this Licence (by Uniform Resource Identifier (URI), spoken word or as appropriate to the media used) on all copies of the Work and Collective Works published, distributed, performed or otherwise disseminated or made available to the public by You;

- recognise the Licensor's/Original Author's rights of attribution in any Work and Collective Work that You publish, distribute, perform or otherwise disseminate to the public and ensure that You credit the Licensor/Original Author as appropriate to the media used; and

- to the extent reasonably practicable, keep intact all notices that refer to this Licence, in particular the URI, if any, that the Licensor specifies to be associated with the Work, unless such URI does not refer to the copyright notice or licensing information for the Work.

Additional Provisions for third parties making use of the Work

2.2   Further licence from the Licensor

Each time You publish, distribute, perform or otherwise disseminate

- the Work; or

- the Work as incorporated in a Collective Work

the Licensor agrees to offer to the relevant third party making use of the Work (in any of the alternatives set out above) a licence to use the Work on the same terms and conditions as granted to You hereunder.

2.3   This Licence deos not affect any rights that the User may have under any applicable law, including fair use, fair delaing or any other legally recognised limitation or exception to copyright infringement.

2.4   All rights not expressly granted by the Licensor are hereby reserved, including but not limited to, the exclusive right to collect, whether individually or via a licensing body, such as a collecting society, royalties for any use of the Work.

3.   Warranties and Disclaimer

Except as required by law, the Work is licensed by the Licensor on an 'as is' and 'as available' basis and without any warranty of any kind, either express or implied.

4.   Limit of Liability

Subject to any liability which may not be excluded or limited by law the Licensor shall not be liable and hereby expressly excludes all liability for loss or damage howsoever and whenever caused to You.

5.   Termination

The rights granted to You under this Licence shall terminate automatically upon any breach by You of the terms of this Licence. Individuals or entities who have received Collective Works from You under this Licence, however will not have their Licences terminated provided such individuals or entities remain in full compliance with those Licences.

6.   General

6.1   The validity or enforcement of the remaining terms of this agreement is not affected by the holding of any provision of it to be invalid or unenforceable.

6.2   This Licence constitutes the entire Licence Agreement between the parties with respect to the Work licensed here. There are no understandings, agreements or representations with respect to the Work not specified here. The Licensor shall not be bound by any additional provisions that may appear in any communication in any form.

6.3   A person who is not a party to this Licence shall have no rights under the Contracts (Rights of Third Parties) Act 1999 to enforce any of its terms.

6.4   This Licence shall be governed by the law of England and Wales and the parties irrevocably submit to the exclusive jurisdiction of the Courts of England and Wales.

7.   On the Role of Creative Commons

7.1   Neither the Licensor nor the User may use the Creative Commons logo except to indicate that the Work is licensed under a Creative Commons Licence. Any permitted use has to be in compliance with the Creative Commons trade mark usage guidelines at the time of use of the Creative Commons trade mark. These guidelines may be found on the Creative Commons website or be otherwise available upon request from time to time.

7.2   Creative Commons Corporation does not profit from its role in providing this Licence and will not investigate the claims of any Licensor or user of the Licence.

7.3   One of the conditions that Creative Commons Corporation requires of the Licensor and You is an acknowledgment of its limited roles and agreement by all who use the Licence that the Corporation is not responsible to anyone for the statements and actions of You or the Licensor or anyone else attempting to use this Licence.

7.4 Creative Commons Corporation is not a party to this Licence, and makes no warranty whatsoever in connection to the Work or in connection to this Licence, and in all events is not liable for any loss or damage resulting from the Licensor's or Your reliance on this Licence or on its enforceability.

7.5 USE OF THIS LICENCE MEANS THAT YOU AND THE LICENSOR EACH ACCEPTS THESE CONDITIONS IN SECTION 7.1, 7.2, 7.3, 7.4 AND EACH ACKNOWLEDGES CREATIVE COMMONS CORPORATION'S VERY LIMITED ROLE AS A FACILITATOR OF THE LICENCE FROM THE LICENSOR TO YOU.

Creative Commons is not a party to this Licence, and makes no warranty whatsoever in connection with the Work. Creative Commons will not be liable to You or any party on any legal theory for any damages whatsoever, including without limitation any general, special, incidental or consequential damages arising in connection to this Licence. Notwithstanding the foregoing two (2) sentences, if Creative Commons has expressly identified itself as the Licensor hereunder, it shall have all rights and obligations of Licensor.

Except for the limited purpose of indicating to the public that the Work is licensed under the CCPL, neither party will use the trademark 'Creative Commons' or any related trademark or logo of Creative Commons without the prior written consent of Creative Commons. Any permitted use will be in compliance with Creative Commons' then current trademark usage guidelines, as may be published on its website or otherwise made available upon request from time to time.

Creative Commons may be contacted at http://creativecommons.org/.

PODCASTING

A very recent development in the sphere of internet communications is the broadcasting of audio files online, dominated by the use of MP3 files. This practice has been dubbed 'podcasting', which can be misleading, given that one does not require an Apple iPod in order to participate. The attraction of making audio files available on a website is that visitors can download them and listen at their own convenience on their PCs or portable players. With the increased availability of broadband permitting faster upload and download speeds, podcasting has come into its own.

Podcast audio files can be used, for example, to provide audio feed with news or updates about a film release in much the same way that websites already provide articles and short news items. In some cases, podcasting has seen the use of portable players to generate film shows which can be accessed as stated at any time by the recipient. Needless to say such broadcasts fall outside the scope of any traditional broadcast regulation.

The process of podcasting is simple, requiring only a good microphone and audio software for recording in the MP3 format. One needs to create a feed with a link to the audio file and upload the file to a website. Making the feed involves using a very short piece of code describing what the audio file is and what it is about. Listeners can either save the files when they visit the website or subscribe to the feed and download them automatically.

On a positive note, the emergence of podcasting might see the development of a genuinely innovative form of mobile broadcast providing an unmatched freedom and interactivity to a new generation of listeners.

POSSIBLE MODELS FOR LEGITIMATE FILM DOWNLOADS

A number of companies offering legitimate music download services have emerged in recent times and appear to be performing very well. On the face of it each of these companies offers identical services. However, there is a variety of business models which also impact on the cost of the downloads.

A subscription service primarily seeks to build a community around its users. For a monthly fee unlimited downloads can be accessed onto the hard drives of a maximum number of PCs. There is a further small fee per file to copy the film to a DVD or transfer to a portable device. The films are downloaded in the encrypted Windows Media Audio format, which can be transferred to different portable players.

Another model is a small fee per file and the files can be shared by a maximum specified number of computers on a network, burnt an unlimited number of times to DVD and copied to an unlimited number of devices. The service involves a single pricing model for its downloads.

The battle for market share in the growth of online film is likely to move to the high street, with a range of high street stores encouraging customers to buy more film content on the internet. These may include a pay-as-you-go system for downloading films as well as a monthly subscription allowing unlimited downloading.

A number of brand name Internet Service Providers are now offering a limited number of free downloads as part of their broadband package.

There is clear evidence that consumers are increasingly accessing their film from the internet but need the encouragement of a trusted brand that can demystify the experience.

INTERNET PROTOCOL TELEVISION (IPTV)

Internet Protocol Television or IPTV is the delivery of digital television and other audio and video services over broadband data networks using the same basic protocols that support the internet. With faster broadband access speeds and improved digital video compression it is possible to deliver high quality video services over the telephone line. A small decoder box can connect a television to a telephone or network point, rather than an aerial socket, cable or satellite feed, and the picture quality is high.

The advent of IPTV opens up the television market to telephone companies and other service providers with lower barriers to entry than existing digital platforms. However, such providers still need to comply with the proposed Audiovisual Services Directive (Chapter 18). Traditional telecommunication companies are keen to augment their diminishing call revenues with new services. They have the opportunity to offer a new, albeit familiar, popular consumer service over their broadband network. One of their main objectives is a triple play of voice, video and data services on a single bill. Although service providers may attempt to bundle television channels and compete directly with cable and satellite companies, once a broadband connection is hooked up to the television, programmes could potentially come from anywhere.

The attraction of IPTV is the fact that it has the ability to completely alter the way that information, communications and media services are consumed inside the home. IPTV moves the television experience from a passive model to an active, two-way communication where every subscriber experience has the potential to be unique. A subscriber can choose to receive only the channels and programmes desired and pay for the content consumed. In addition the user can, perhaps, send an instant message to a friend about the latest developments on a favourite show while both are watching it in their respective homes. Alternatively, they might be able to change the camera angle while watching a live concert or sporting event. IPTV allows the provider to offer personalised content (Chapter 7), targeted information and shopping experiences and more targeted advertising (Chapter 12).

There are opportunities for media content owners and film companies as the telecommunication companies have little experience in dealing with media companies and content aggregators who own the distribution rights. Film companies may be able to demand minimum levels of subscribers as part of any deal and an attractive royalty split. As with all other new media opportunities discussed in this book, the potential for IPTV is yet unknown, but many in the new media industry believe that strong content is the key to success. This will enable the IPTV service provider to set a price and bundle services which are attractive to subscribers and profitable to the provider. It will also ensure that advertisers are attracted to the medium.

IPTV will allow normally unserviceable niche audiences to be reached by media companies. Entertainment will not be the preserve of the broadcasters and Internet Service Providers will be able to commission, produce and distribute entertainment media. IPTV is not simply viewed on PCs but also on mobile phones. IPTV can also be used for non-commercial home monitoring and localised news services.

For any film company that considers establishing its own IPTV service, all the issues addressed in this book will impact on the service to varying degrees and comprehensive new media legal advice should be taken.

CHECKLIST

- Ensure that the film company understands fully the 'making available right' and that the film website fulfils the requirements of the Copyright and Related Rights Regulations 2003.

- Consider whether adoption of the Creative Commons Licence is appropriate to the film company's online activity.

CHAPTER 6

The Marketing of Film and Merchandise Online

THE PRIVACY AND ELECTRONIC COMMUNICATIONS (EC DIRECTIVE) REGULATIONS 2003

INTRODUCTION

It is very difficult to get films marketed and distributed. Films only have a value if there is a market. The key to driving audiences is to apply the standard of getting people out of the comfort of their own homes on a wet Wednesday night to visit the cinema. Therefore the content has to be of a high quality. That quality level applies with equal force to any film business wishing to produce and distribute their content online even though the audience need never leave their living room.

However, there are clear differences in approach between traditional promotion and online marketing. We are entering an era of content abundance, which is the internet. This is contrasted with the world of cinema, which is about scarcity. For example, Odeon Cinemas have around 900 screens in the UK and account for one in three of all cinema tickets sold in this country.

The internet is just another shop window for filmmakers to get their content into. As the PC leaves the bedroom in most people's homes to move into the living room and as those PCs become more media centre than IT device, the internet thus changes the environment in which we consume television and film.

Although there are opportunities for content owners to maximise exposure to their target markets using the internet in many ways there is no less effort required. Whereas traditional methods of signing a sales agent or distributor for the film inevitably involves a revenue share arrangement, undertaking direct promotion as content owner requires immediate and significant commercial effort. The content owner has to reach out to their e-mail database and find their audience online. Whilst they may not have to convince one individual in a studio to take their film but instead make the film available online to a potentially vast audience themselves, there is a huge amount of careful marketing preparation and maintenance associated with direct film promotion.

The increase in the sophistication of apparatus in the telecommunications sector in recent years is tremendous. In particular, mobile phones have evolved to the extent that they no longer merely serve as voice data instruments permitting telephone conversations from wherever there exists a service. Mobiles enable photographs to be taken and instantly e-mailed to other mobile subscribers. Internet access is possible and with the rapid growth of 3G services video downloads and broadcast material are accessible directly via the mobile phone. They are a modern day marvel.

The marketing industry recognises the potential for mobile phones as highly advanced marketing tools. The attraction rests in the ability to contact the subscriber directly, regardless of location. Mobile phones and handheld devices offer all the benefits of the internet without the major hurdle of being restricted to sitting in front of a computer. The appeal of offering film, or more likely film trailers, via mobile apparatus is heightened by the uptake of 3G which not only speeds up mobile access to the internet but also provides handsets with faster processors and, crucially, larger screens that make watching film trailer videos available to a wider audience. The interest in using mobile phones as a means of selling goods and services is enhanced with the possibility of location-based services. For example, a film DVD retailer based in a shopping mall or perhaps exhibiting at a film festival can send a text or e-mail to the mobile phone of those people in the vicinity of the shop or stand offering a discount on DVDs for the first 100 visitors. The message is only received by the subscriber if they are within a defined radius but one can see how powerful the sales potential is in the use of such sophisticated technology.

Most film fans searching for information or merchandise relating to a new film release or their favourite films do not necessarily search the internet under the name of the film production company. It is likely the fan does not care which production company or distributor the film is released through. They will search using the title name or an actor's name. In the early days of the internet, film production company websites tended to be principally corporate information sites providing details for the benefit of other companies. Today film company websites are far more orientated towards a magazine format offering latest news on their scheduled releases, current productions and details of their back catalogue. Usually the website will be linked to another website perhaps owned by the film distributors. Another likely link might be to another organisation providing merchandise in relation to the films. In the first section of Chapter 11 we examine how a strategic link between a film company and a computer games developer offering an online game designed around the title would be regulated by a formal Linking Agreement. Film businesses now provide a vast array of deals on their websites designed to support the promotion of their titles. The attraction of the internet as a medium for such activity is the ability to interact with the website visitor in a manner hitherto not possible.

Film websites can provide film companies with information about their audiences which they could not gather by any other means. Websites can serve as points of contact through which personal data about the filmgoer can be ascertained. This might include age, gender and location, including country of residence. We examine in Chapter 7 how film companies must abide by the requirements of the Data Protection Act 1998 when they gather and maintain such information. Websites offer the company an ability to interact with the filmgoers in real time and to offer time-specific deals to those who can enter online competitions, communicate live with those associated with the production and purchase merchandise on a special offer for, say, a limited number of hours. Film companies can use their websites as a means of offering additional information to audiences that they could not otherwise obtain. When one considers the degree of sophistication with which a film business can market and promote its titles using the internet, one can understand why those in the industry place great emphasis on their websites. Film companies will therefore want to either own or control title websites and domain names.

Branding of film and television titles has never been more popular and commercially attractive. There has been huge interest in television formats that allow the public to vote for would-be stage stars and effectively create media careers almost overnight. These interactive television programmes are always supported by websites which also offer the ability to vote in the contest. The websites can also offer a glimpse of the inside story and behind the scenes activity of the contestants as the competition develops. Given that many of these performers will enjoy fame for a comparatively short period, the need to maximise earnings through as many media as possible is clear. The internet provides this possibility and the interactive nature and convergence with television has spawned a new genre of programming. The success of this branding frenzy rests also with the deployment of as many media technology outlets as possible. The increasingly sophisticated mobile phone and its appeal to the youth market offers just such an outlet.

Despite a slow start the growth in mobile phone marketing is now apparent and its relationship to film promotion is clear. First, mobile subscriptions are approaching 100 per cent saturation in the UK and will exceed that as individuals begin to use more than one mobile phone. The apparatus itself has become a fashion item and has obvious appeal to a youth market. The same age demographic tends to be those who are interested in film releases and as such have a demand for merchandise that promotes the title. The phones have colour screen capacity offering the ability to view video content. The film business can appreciate that, with clever data collection, it can deliver real time video content direct to the consumer's mobile phone based on their age, gender and genre preference. The key to this marketing nirvana lies in the collection and retention of that data.

In many ways the reaction to mobile marketing is defined by generation. For many people who did not grow up with mobile phones the thought of being bombarded with marketing messages wherever they might happen to be is appalling. However, to a generation that does not know life without mobile communication it is probably a natural state of affairs and as consumers with spending power they have no objection to the trend.

Nonetheless, regulators soon appreciated that there must be sensible control over the use of people's personal information and the way a company could obtain and then commence transmission to someone's mobile phone number. The whole question once again turns on the issue of data protection and in order to protect the privacy of mobile subscribers it would prove necessary to introduce a set of laws which would make clear what is and what is not acceptable.

Given the significant adoption of mobile phone technology by the film industry it is important to review the laws that must be adhered to in this area. In this section, we make frequent use of examples and characterise the business for the purpose of illustration as a film company or business. This term could include a production company, sales agent, distributor or any other business associated with the film world and as such will be used as a generic term.

As we will see in Chapter 7, the legislation that governs the use of personally identifiable information relating to individuals in the UK is the Data Protection Act 1998. The principles contained in that Act must still be met by a film business wishing to develop a marketing campaign targeted at its e-mail and mobile phone consumer database. However, in addition to the Act the film company must also abide by the provisions of the *Privacy and Electronic Communications (EC Directive) Regulations 2003*.

The need for and the introduction of regulations highlight the problem lawmakers face in the world where media technology is developing so quickly.

In 1999, for example – hardly an age ago and certainly not ancient by legislative standards – regulations were introduced to control the unfettered use of telephone numbers by businesses wishing to sell to consumers. Those regulations were the Telecommunications (Data Protection and Privacy) Regulations 1999. In the short period following their adoption e-mail use and mobile phone adoption has been such that it clearly became necessary to revisit the issue of control and come up with a new set of rules more suited to the reality of the marketplace. The result, following a good deal of consultation with industry and consumer groups alike is the Privacy and Electronic Communications (EC Directive) Regulations 2003.

The Regulations came into effect in the UK on 11 December 2003. It is important to emphasise that, given their nature as Regulations, they are common to the rest of the European Union. As such, however, their ambit extends only throughout the member states and they do not and cannot govern activity generated outside the EU.

In our review of the Regulations it is important to make clear that we are referring to not only voice data telephone calls (telephone conversations), but also SMS text messages, e-mail and other electronic messaging.

Regulation 4 of the new Regulations make clear that they do not relieve a person of any obligations under the Data Protection Act 1998.

TRAFFIC DATA

Regulations 7 and 8 set out certain restrictions on the processing of traffic data relating to a subscriber or user by a telecommunications provider. When one considers the issue it can be appreciated that the study of actual user data can reveal how the subscriber uses their mobile phone. This is useful to mobile phone service providers so that they can market appropriate tariffs to their subscribers. It would also be of interest to those marketing other services, that is, third party companies wishing to sell other goods and services.

'Traffic data' is defined as 'any data processed for the purpose of the conveyance of a communication or an electronic communications network or for the billing in respect of that communication'. 'Public communications provider' is defined as 'a provider of a public electronic communications network or a public electronic communications service'.

If we consider traffic data from the perspective of a film business wishing to market and promote its content via a mobile phone network in order to get to potential consumer purchasers, the following explanation is helpful.

Regulation 7 says that traffic data relating to a subscriber or user may be processed and stored by a provider of a public electronic communications service in certain circumstances. Remember, we are not talking about third party organisations here, only the phone service provider.

They may process and store the data if it is:

a)   for the purposes of marketing electronic communications services; or

b)   for the provision of value added services to that subscriber; or

c)   if the subscriber has given his consent to the processing or storage; and finally

d)   if the processing or storage is done only for the duration necessary for the marketing of their services or provision of their value added services.

The phone subscriber must be told by the film company about the kind of information which the traffic data will consist of and the duration of such processing before his or her consent is given.

The processing considered above can only be done for the following purposes:

a)   the management of billing or traffic;

b)   customer enquiries;

c)   the prevention or detection of fraud;

d)   the marketing of electronic communications services; or

e)   the provision of value added services.

So the sophistication that traffic data afford a marketer is restricted only to the phone service provider. It cannot be made available to, for example, a film company wishing to tailor its marketing message according to how their film audience actually uses their mobile phone.

Regulation 10 is a provision relevant to film businesses who obtain the mobile number of their target consumer by following the appropriate procedure detailed later in this section. It says that the provider of a public electronic communications service shall provide users originating a call with a simple means to prevent presentation of the identity of the calling line on the connected line with respect to that call. Thus, the calling film business could take up this facility so that the consumer would not necessarily know the identity of the company. This service must be provided free by the company providing the phone service.

LOCATION DATA

Let us now consider the matter of location data. We stated earlier that the use of location-based services by a film company was possible. Suppose the film company wishes to provide value-added services to the mobile phone consumer via a network and it strikes an agreement with the network provider to offer certain services or merchandise. Which rules must the film company and the phone company provider adhere to when offering such a service?

The Regulations state at 14(2) that location data relating to a user may only be processed where that user cannot be identified from such data or where necessary for the provision of a value-added service with the consent of that user or subscriber.

Before obtaining the consent of the subscriber the phone company must provide the following information to the subscriber:

a)   the types of location data that will be processed;

b)   the purposes and duration of the processing of the data;

c)   whether the data will be transmitted to a third party for the purpose of providing the value-added service.

The subscriber can withdraw his or her consent at any time, free of charge.

The said processing of the location data can only be carried out by:

a)   the public communications provider in question;

b)   the third party (for example, a film company) providing the value-added service in question; or

c)   a person acting under the authority of either of the above.

Suppose the film business wants to set up an automated calling system to contact its target consumer audience. The Regulations also set out how this process must be conducted. Regulation 19(2) states that the phone subscriber must have previously given his or her consent to such communications being sent.

UNSOLICITED TEXT MESSAGING FOR DIRECT MARKETING PURPOSES

We now turn to the rules that must be followed strictly if a film business wishes to contact consumers with a view to marketing or promoting its titles. First, let us consider this process assuming the film company wishes to do this on an unsolicited basis using, for example, the mobile phone number of the subscriber.

The Regulations provide for two mechanisms by which the consumer can ensure that no unsolicited phone calls are made to their number. First, the person may have notified the film company that no such calls should be made to that number. Second, and more likely, the consumer may have registered their phone number with the Telephone Preference Service. This is a register maintained by OFCOM which contains the numbers of individuals who do not wish to receive any unsolicited phone calls.

Provided the consumer has neither notified the film company of their objection to marketing calls nor registered with the Telephone Preference Service, it is possible for the company to make unsolicited calls to that individual. Remember, the definition of 'calls' includes both voice data and SMS text messages.

Thus, the rules for making speech calls to a target consumer or indeed sending them a text message are clear. However, with convergence of technology many mobile phones also have the capacity to send and receive e-mail communications. The Regulations also contain rules concerning use of e-mail for marketing purposes.

There was a great deal of consultation by the UK government before the Regulations were introduced. The concern was to ensure that the proper balance between fair activities of the marketing community and the legitimate needs of consumers to maintain privacy was maintained. It must be understood that the Regulations only apply in the context of business-to-consumer relationships. That is, they apply solely to situations where a business, such as a film company, wishes to make unsolicited telephone calls or send unsolicited e-mails to a target consumer. The Regulations do not apply to the situation where that business wishes to market its services to another business. This was largely due to the fact that businesses expect to be marketed to and to impose a bar on marketing calls and e-mails would run counter to the spirit of enterprise. However, the government made it clear that if the evidence over the following few years pointed to business-to-business unsolicited communications becoming a significant menace then further regulation would be considered with a view to combating the problem.

The other point to emphasise is that these laws can only address the problem of unsolicited messages if they originate from within the EU. The rules do provide a framework for film businesses in terms of how they must go about marketing their titles and associated merchandise using electronic communications. The Regulations have been successful in controlling what was fast becoming a major problem. They cannot, however, govern film companies based outside the EU. Therefore such businesses can still send unsolicited communications to consumers and, of course, other businesses without restriction. This is why many readers will doubtless receive several e-mails a day from businesses based, for example, in the United States of America.

There are exceptions to the general bar as a film company on sending unsolicited e-mails to consumers.

If the film company can demonstrate that one of the following conditions has been satisfied then it will not be deemed to have infringed the Regulations.

Regulation 22(3) states that:

A person may send or instigate the sending of electronic mail for the purposes of direct marketing where–

(a) *that person has obtained the contact details of the recipient of that electronic mail in the course of the sale or negotiations for the sale of a product or service to that recipient;*

(b) *the direct marketing is in respect of that person's similar products and services only; and*

(c) *the recipient has been given a simple means of refusing (free of charge except for the costs of the transmission of the refusal) the use of his contact details for the purposes of such direct marketing, at the time that the details were initially collected, and, where he did not initially refuse the use of the details, at the time of each subsequent communication.*

These exceptions allow for a degree of flexibility on the part of a film company which intends to market its titles and merchandise. For example, (a) might be satisfied if the consumer has previously given their contact details to the company as part of a promotional offer or competition. It might be that the film company offered a prize of premier theatre tickets, inviting people to enter the competition and asking them to complete their address details. Any contact details thus obtained would permit the film company to commence sending e-mails to those individuals without infringing the Regulations. The second exception, (b), is also fairly wide. In the case of a supermarket selling a wide range of product it might be difficult for them to start marketing film DVD titles to their consumer database when those consumers have only previously purchased groceries. However, in the case of a film company it might be that it has previously sold music DVDs to its consumers but now wishes to offer film DVDs or perhaps a film download service. Such offers would amount to similar goods or services and therefore the film company would not infringe the Regulations.

The third exception deals with the situation in which a consumer has notified his or her willingness to receive future marketing communications. The individual has to 'opt in' to the receipt of such messages. In the past a marketing department could regard an individual's silence as acceptance. Thus, the film company could draft a response form for the consumer to complete which required the consumer to tick a box to indicate their objection to receiving material in the future ('opt out'). If the consumer did not tick that box the company was entitled to assume that consent had been granted and they could continue to send material. The Regulations now require the consumer to tick expressly that they have no objection to receiving marketing communications.

If a film company wishes to instigate a publicity and marketing campaign using electronic communications it must follow the above procedures. It should also state clearly the precise means by which it might market its merchandise or services to the target consumer in the future. Thus, if it intends to send SMS text message to the individual's phone, this must be made clear. If in addition or as an alternative it wants to send e-mails, this must be clarified.

One interesting point of note is that, as we have said, the Regulations only apply to individuals. However, the definition of individuals also includes 'an unincorporated body of such individuals' which could include a legal partnership.

Another important restriction on a tactic that might be thought useful is contained in Regulation 23. This prohibits the sending of communications by means of e-mail for the purposes of direct marketing where the identity of the person on whose behalf the communication is made has been disguised or concealed or an address to which requests for such communications to cease may be sent has not been provided.

The important thing to note is that a film company cannot seek to exclude a consumer's rights under the Regulations by contractual term. So, for example, in the website terms and conditions (Chapter 3) the film company could not include a clause which informed their online consumer that they could expect to receive future marketing communications without offering that person the ability to register their express consent.

There are penalties which will be imposed on a film company which infringes the Regulations. Regulation 30 allows a claim for damages to be brought by the person receiving the messages. The film company can mount a defence if it can prove it took such care as in all the circumstances was reasonably required to comply with the relevant requirement.

The Regulations also add an obligation on those film companies who wish to use cookies or other similar software tracking devices to notify their use to their online consumer. A cookie is an electronic tag which permits website operators to identify the buying habits of their online consumers. They allow for very sophisticated marketing. They are widely deployed on commercial retail websites and they make possible the suggestion of similar film titles of likely interest to the website visitor. Internet users will be familiar with such technology if, for example, they use Amazon to purchase film DVDs. The Regulations do not forbid the use of such technology in a website but the film company must include a clause in its website terms and conditions notifying the visitor to the website that the site uses cookies for these purposes.

For a film company, the dawn of mobile marketing combines the wide reach of television with the precision of direct marketing and the tracking potential of the internet with massive publicity and advertising cost savings. Some in the new media sphere believe that the mobile phone could become one of the most important media for advertisers and marketers. The mobile phone industry actually has a huge market advantage in the new media world in that phone companies already have a ready-made single billing system for their subscribers. Those subscribers expect to pay for content such as music ringtones. Therefore, for the film company wishing to access new markets using new media, the approach to mobile phone service providers is perhaps a route to consider.

In the initial phase of mobile marketing some major brands ran mobile campaigns which were usually one-off pilots with little long-term commitment. More recently companies have taken the medium more seriously and the film industry is an obvious participant. The potential for film content to be marketed via mobile phones has been ushered in by two principal factors: first, fast networks and high functionality phones and second, the sheer ubiquity and importance of the mobile phone among consumers. Indeed, some research suggests that people were more willing to do without television than their mobile phones. The evidence also suggests that on returning from school or college, children and young people do not switch on the television but rather log on to the internet. The world that the media industry understands is rapidly changing. Audiences are becoming fractured.

The devices, of course, do more than facilitate voice calls. In 2004 26 billion text messages were sent in the United Kingdom. With the ability to send content-rich messages made possible by 3G, film companies can appreciate that mobile phones must become a part of their promotional portfolio. Strategic mobile marketing should be seen as part of their mix of communication strategy. In addition, mobile phone service providers can enter into the film services domain by offering film and television content via their network. Such services have already begun to have an impact on the youth market for phones. The possibilities for delivering appealing media content to mobiles are tremendous.

The mobile phone service providers are becoming primary portals for the filmmaker. The film producer needs to think in terms of approaches to service providers which ensure that the producer has the kind of titles the provider can find a market for and which will drive market share for the mobile phone provider. However, at the time of writing there are still inhibitors to the technology and thus its attraction to the film industry. For any technology to become mass market it has to be universal. At present 3G is not. Handset penetration has a significant way to go and interoperability is also acting as an impediment to growth.

Film companies need to integrate mobile phones into their content. It is almost certain that filmmakers will need to create content according to platform – for example, for online download, mobile phone view and other media. This might require different versions of the same content being adapted according to platform.

The music industry has seen its business model change radically as a consequence of the internet but has apparently won the battle. For example, it is now common for a record company to offer music ringtones of tracks featured on a new album release. The user simply sends a text message to a specified number code and for around £3 they can obtain a polythonic ringtone. The film business needs to similarly re-engineer itself for the online era.

It is thus useful to consider how a film company might go about marketing its titles and supporting merchandise by the use of mobile phones. As we have seen, the telephone service provider can use the traffic and billing data it holds about its subscribers for the purpose of marketing further services to them. It cannot release that data to a third party company but it can, however, release the mobile phone number of a subscriber to a third party company such as a film company, where the telephone service company has included a clause in its network access contract with the subscriber. That clause might state that the film company is entitled to release numbers to third party companies with a view to those companies sending marketing messages.

If the mobile phone service provider has included this notification then the film company might acquire (for a fee) that database of mobile phone numbers. However, the film company would then have to send an initial message to the subscriber stating that they intend to send marketing messages in the future and the means by which those messages will be sent. This is known as a Data Protection Notice. The subscriber must then expressly signify their agreement to receiving those messages. This acceptance might be given by visiting the film company's website to register consent. Provided the subscriber does give consent in this way the film company can commence marketing its products and services to the mobile phone subscriber. The subscriber can refuse their consent at any time and, if so notified, the film company must cease transmission of material or face legal penalties.

CHECKLIST

The 2003 Regulations changed the previous rules in the following ways:

1   They replace the previous definitions for telecommunications services and networks with new definitions for electronic communications and services to ensure technological neutrality and clarify the position of e-mail and use of the internet.

2   They enable the provision of value-added services based on location and traffic data, subject to the consent of subscribers (for example, location-based advertising to mobile phone users).

3   They remove the possibility of a subscriber being charged for exercising the right not to appear in public directories.

4   They introduce new information and consent requirements on entries in publicly available directories, including a requirement that subscribers are informed of all the usage possibilities of publicly available directories, for example, reverse searching from a telephone number in order to obtain a name and address.

5   They extend controls on unsolicited direct marketing to all forms of electronic communications including unsolicited commercial e-mail (spam) and SMS to mobile telephones.

6   They introduce controls on the use of cookies on websites.

CHAPTER 7

Collecting Online Data about Film-buying Audiences

PRIVACY CONSIDERATIONS WITH ONLINE FILM

The principal attraction of the internet is that it is an open environment. It is the superdistribution channel of the modern age and lends itself spectacularly well to media distribution. Audiences are becoming forms of community and people are consuming media in more and more contexts. Internet audiences are more fragmented but equally online viewers leave a more visible footprint about their interests, dreams and desires. The key is identifying that audience so that content can be targeted precisely.

One area which offers huge opportunity for a film company is the increasingly sophisticated means by which personal information about the consumer audience can be obtained. The richness of the content of this data and how it may be measured is simply incredible and was not possible only a few years ago.

The pace of change is staggering. Most recently, social networking websites have shown the potential for internet film distribution. The success of sites such as MySpace and FaceBook depend on users putting up online a whole range of information about themselves and what they do. The ability to use this information and share it with others is a significant aspect of both the business model and the attraction of the site. At the same time, content owners cannot quarantine the viral video outbreak but instead can use the websites to spark interest in their underlying programmes by making clips available. But such sites bring with them issues of data protection, data security and data sharing. Social networking websites, however, are just one aspect of the issue of data collection online.

To ensure the success of any online film application, whether it is the offer of physical film DVDs and other merchandise over the internet or the making available of online film downloads, it is important that the company can target its users properly. However, the internet does not exist in a legal vacuum. In the European Union at least it resides in a heavily regulated data protection regime. In this chapter we will examine why privacy laws have huge significance in relation to the internet and mobile telephone use by film companies.

The sheer wealth and diversity of its content encourages the immediate, though often transient, review of a host of published data. There are legitimate concerns by consumers over marketers buying and selling their personal information. The rise of e-commerce has sparked increasing fears because of the ease with which all types of sensitive data may be gathered, copied, shared and misused via the internet.

It is vital that a film company understands how it may operate safely and adhere to the legal protection afforded to individuals in the European Union. Moreover, given the pan-national nature of the internet, the company needs to know how it can process personal information in a way which does not fall foul of the data protection regime of other countries.

These problems are particularly acute for film companies with an international reach. In addition to possible fines there is a risk of negative publicity for breaching data protection laws. No company can afford to ignore the issues.

It is necessary to examine the basis of data protection principles as they apply within the EU and to consider how they relate to a film company's use of the internet and mobile communications apparatus. In addition, the rules for transfer of data from the United Kingdom (and indeed from any country in the EU) to a country outside the EU will be explained.

It is fair to say that the EU has one of the most stringent data protection regimes in the world. Some feel that there is a lack of connection between this restricted approach and the realities of the global nature of the internet. The information-gathering ability of companies has caused concerns over invasion of citizens' rights for many years. In most countries, the unlawful processing of personal data represents a violation of fundamental human rights.

In the United Kingdom company directors are personally liable for the accuracy of their organisations' databases. Individuals can sue not merely for financial loss directly resulting from inaccurate or wrongly disclosed data, but also for any breach of data law and resultant distress.

To view the signifance of the data protection rules to a film company's existing or planned online operations, one need only consider that a commercial website which is run by a film company might well sell film in physical or digital download form as well as other merchandise. The information superhighway collects, processes and transfers a prodigious amount of personal data. When purchasing from a website, the online customer will of necessity disclose their home address, contact details, credit card information and other personal information. Confidence that the film company will maintain that data responsibly is vital. For example, a film company might wish to develop new methods of earning revenue. The internet enables film companies to monitor profiles and information provided directly by its online audience. The process of tracking every click the consumer makes on the internet and leaving behind 'cookies' on their computers to help the system remember each consumer is hugely valuable. Companies can gather a startling amount of personal information with which to sell consumers film merchandise and services. The vast majority of commercial websites are dependent on cookies to customise the site to users' preferences: without them sites become almost unusable.

An example of the technology lies in a purchase of a DVD on Amazon.com. In time, the site will begin to suggest new purchases each time the consumer visits, based on the buying pattern that individual has established.

The argument in favour of online marketing is that it helps consumers find the right products efficiently and conveniently. There are controls on the use of cookies contained within the Privacy and Electronic Communications Regulations 2003, as we have seen in Chapter 6. However, since many browsers allow users to block cookies and to delete them from their PCs, a criticism has been levelled at Europe. It is suggested that user awareness about the use of cookies rather than legal constraint is the preferable approach. The contrary view is that such ability creates many new ways for highly personal data to be misused or stolen.

THE DATA PROTECTION ACT 1998

In the UK the law which governs the processing of personal data is embodied in the Data Protection Act 1998 (the Act), which came into force on 1 March 2000. It replaced the Data Protection Act 1984 and it implements the principles of EU Directive 95/46/EC.

In 1995 the European Parliament and Council issued the EU Directive on Data Protection (96.46/EEC). The Directive sought to protect individuals with regard to the processing of personal data and free movement of such data. The Directive led to the introduction of the 1998 Act, which is more extensive than the 1984 legislation. Whilst the Act sets forth the overall legal framework, much of the detail is contained in secondary legislation.

The most significant difference to previous legislation is the new definition of 'processing'. This is defined as 'obtaining, recording or holding the information or data or carrying out any operation or set of operations on the information or data'. Thus, for a film company – particularly those which make extensive use the internet or indeed IT generally to run their business process – the Act imposes a significant compliance programme.

The Act applies in the following circumstances:

1   If the film company is 'established' in the UK, that is, it is ordinarily resident, a UK limited company, partnership or unincorporated business. In addition, the Act applies if that business has an office, branch or agency that carries on any activity in the UK.

2   If the film company is not established in the UK but uses equipment in this country for processing data.

3   If data is exported to the film company from the UK.

As is the case with much of the law relating to online film strategies featured in this book, there is correspondent legislation in place throughout the EU, subject only to minor variation.

The information covered by the legislation is 'personal data',that is, data relating to a living individual who can be identified directly or indirectly. Employees, suppliers, customers and business contacts all fall within the definition.

THE EIGHT DATA PROTECTION PRINCIPLES

The 1998 Act and related EU regulation set out eight principles which organisations must follow:

1   All personal data which is held must be processed fairly and lawfully. It must not be processed unless one of the conditions at schedule (2) is met. More stringent conditions apply to the processing of sensitive personal data. These are set out in Schedule 3 to the 1998 Act. The Act defines 'sensitive personal data' as 'personal data consisting of information as to a data subject's racial or ethnic origin, political opinions, religious beliefs, or other beliefs of a similar nature. Membership of a trade union, physical or mental health or condition, sexual life, or commission or alleged commission or proceedings in relation to any of them.

Processing sensitive data will only be legitimate if the data subject has given his or her 'explicit consent'. If sensitive personal data is used, at least one condition at Schedule 3 must also be met. It is clear that personal data will not be considered to be processed 'fairly' unless certain information is provided, or made readily available to the individual concerned.

The information to be given to data subjects must include the identity of the data controller, the purposes for which the data is intended to be processed and any further information which is necessary having regard to the specific circumstances in which the data is to be processed, to enable processing in respect of the data subject to be fair. Where data is obtained directly from the data subject, the requisite information should normally be provided at, or be made available from, the time of data collection.

2   Personal data shall only be obtained for one or more specified and lawful purpose. It should not be further processed in a manner incompatible with that purpose.

3   Personal data must be adequate, relevant and not excessive in relation to the purpose for which it is processed. Whilst an online enquirer might, in the course of a transaction, be willing to give a film company a great deal of personal information, that business has a duty to protect enquirers from themselves and their generosity. Clearly this has implications for data collection by a film company via the internet. Many websites require regular visitors to register before gaining access. It is very important that the film company makes clear precisely why non-essential questions are being asked and whether a response is optional. For example, capturing an e-mail address may be necessary for the provision of a particular service, whereas collecting information about gender, marital status, income and age may be irrelevant or excessive.

4   Personal data must be accurate and kept up to date where necessary.

5   Personal data processed for any purpose shall not be kept for longer than is necessary for that purpose.

6   Personal data must be processed in accordance with the rights of data subjects under the Act.

7   Appropriate technological and organisational measures will be taken against unauthorised or unlawful processing of personal data. Such action will also be taken in the case of accidental loss, destruction or damage to personal data.

This principle needs to be considered carefully by the film company. If the film company uses a data processor such as an Internet Service Provider (ISP) or other third party which processes data on its behalf – for example, by hosting the website – it will be in breach of this seventh principle unless both of the following criteria are satisfied:

i)   the processor provides sufficient guarantees in respect of the technical and organisational security measures governing the processing to be carried out, and the film company takes reasonable steps to ensure compliance with those measures;

ii)   the processing is governed by a written contract requiring the processor to act only as instructed by the controller and to comply with security obligations equivalent to those imposed in the controller. In the context of the internet, the film company will therefore need to ensure it has appropriate and properly documented contractual arrangements in place with, amongst others, its ISP and website hosters.

EXPORTING DATA FROM THE UK TO A COUNTRY OUTSIDE THE EU: THE EIGHTH DATA PROTECTION PRINCIPLE AND TRANSBORDER DATA FLOWS

There is one facet of privacy legislation which causes some confusion and can easily be overlooked by a film company, in particular film businesses with an international dimension to their operation. The problem is particularly manifest in the context of electronic communications. The ease with which information can be passed around the globe at the press of a button is contributing to the widespread oversight of the laws which control export of personal data. In many ways the enabling technology which permits the easy transfer of information is to blame, in that the effortless process does not prompt an investigation of the law which controls the action.

The Act introduces a new principle. It prohibits the transfer of personal data outside the EU unless there is an adequate level of protection in the receiving country, or the individual concerned has consented to the transfer.

There are a number of factors which determine the adequacy of legislation in other legal jurisdictions. These include the purpose for which data will be used and the risk involved. There is a problem. Few countries outside the EU in fact operate adequate data protection provisions. Since the internet permits the global transfer of data monitoring of data flow is difficult thereby exacerbating the problem. First it is necessary to consider the broad ambit of the Act.

A film company might infringe the law relating to export of personal information in ways quite common to everyday business operation. For example, the use of information collected as a result of online ordering to send offers of merchandise to existing online customers worldwide. This is the kind of activity which is undertaken daily by film companies in this country.

The legal basis of control lies within the Act. Section 4(4) of the Act provides that '… it shall be the duty of a data controller to comply with the data protection principles in relation to all personal data with respect to which he is the data controller'.

It is the Eighth Principle which governs trans-border data flows that is relevant here. The Eighth Principle states:

> *Personal data shall not be transferred to a country or territory outside*
> *the European Economic Area unless that country or territory ensures*
> *an adequate level of protection for the rights and freedoms of data*
> *subjects in relation to the processing of personal data.*

The European Economic Area consists of the 27 EU member states together with Iceland, Liechtenstein and Norway. The Eighth Principle prohibits the transfer of personal data to any country or territory outside the EEA, a so-called 'third country', unless the third country in question ensures this 'adequate level of protection for the rights and freedoms of data subjects' for transfers of their personal data to such countries. The Act does not define 'transfer' but the ordinary meaning of the word is transmission from one place or person to another. It is important to appreciate that transfer does not mean the same as mere transit. Thus, the fact the electronic transfer of, for example, a film-buying consumer database may be routed through a third country on its way from the UK to another EEA country does not bring such transfer within the ambit of the Eighth Principle unless some substantive processing operation was being conducted on the personal data in the third country in question. A film company can fall within the ambit of the restriction very easily without realising it – if information is provided by, for example, the marketing manager in a film company in the UK over the telephone to his or her counterpart in a third country, who then enters the information on a computer, the legislation will be breached. Another problem area would be mass data transfers from computer to computer using telecommunications systems.

'Processing' is widely defined by the Act and includes the obtaining, using, recording or holding of information, as well as adaptation or retrieval and disclosure of data. In effect, the obligations and principles apply to almost any use or collection of data regarding an individual. Certain information is classified as 'sensitive', and there are additional obligations in relation to sensitive personal data. If the film company wished to include data regarding its consumers' racial or ethnic origin, political beliefs, religious beliefs or sex life these are regarded as sensitive. A UK film company intending to transfer data to a third country must assess the question of adequacy. To most companies, these will appear convoluted. In assessing adequacy the data controller in the film company is required to make a judgement as to whether the level of protection afforded by all the circumstances of the case is commensurate with the potential of personal risks to the rights and freedoms of its consumer database (the data subjects) in relation to the processing of personal data. There are detailed guidelines which assist all companies in making the assessment and in adhering to good practice. These are too numerous to detail for the purposes of this book. There are, however, several forms of international transfer which have been identified by the Confederation of British Industry (CBI) where it may be possible for exporting controllers to approach the adequacy test with a strong presumption in favour of adequacy in terms of assessing the risk involved in the transfer. In the context of a film company these might include:

- transfers to a third party processor who remains under the control of the exporting data controller in the film company;

- transfers within an international or multi-national film business or group of film businesses where an internal agreement, policy or code is more appropriate than a potentially large number of contracts;

- transfers between the providers of professional services such as lawyers or accountants whose clients' affairs are international in scope;

- transfers which amount to a licence for use and probably a rental payment in respect of personal data used, for instance, in direct marketing; and

- transfers which constitute a sale of data to a third party where there is no continuing relationship either with the data subject or the purchaser.

All member states in the EU must take the measures necessary to prevent any transfer of data of the same type to the country in question where the European Commission finds no adequate level of data protection exists. The market for artists in the United States is of particular relevance to a film company. However, the USA is deemed to be a country where no adequate level of protection exists. Thus, if the film company wishes to transfer data from the UK to the USA, two methods of data transfer have been developed – the so-called 'safe harbor' and the EU model clauses. There is a number of alternative options.

First, signing up to the US Privacy Safe Harbor will legitimise transfers to the USA. A second route to compliance is by putting in place contracts between the exporting film business and the importing business. This is a common route to compliance within a corporate group. However, the standard terms that must be included might not prove palatable to many film companies, given how weighted they are in favour of the individual consumer. A third option to addressing transfer may be developing as a variant to a contract on the European Commission's approved terms. In the UK at least it is open to a film company to adopt a policy on privacy compliance which is applicable throughout the company. This policy might be sufficient to address transfer issues provided the policy is binding. This means some form of external dispute resolution mechanism. However, this can be drafted more favourably to the film company than the equivalent provisions in the European Commission's approved terms.

THE UNITED STATES SAFE HARBOR PROCEDURE

US Safe Harbor was the result of five years of negotiation between the US Department of Commerce and the European Commission, resulting in the adoption of a decision regarding Safe Harbor principles. The principles came into effect on 1 November 2000. It is intended to ensure the adequate level of privacy necessary to allow transfers of data from the EU to the USA. Essentially, Safe Harbor provides a set of privacy principles which replicate the data protection principles enshrined in the EU data protection regime. These include:

- notice (of intended use and intended recipients and of how to limit use and make enquiries and complaints);
- choice (both opting out and opting in);
- security;
- data integrity;

- data subject access rights;

- enforcement mechanisms (including effective follow-up procedures).

It is important to emphasise that Safe Harbor only applies between the EU and the US. It is a fair to say that the reaction of most businesses in the USA to the Safe Harbor principles has been unenthusiastic. Comparatively few US corporations have notified the Department of Commerce that they adhere to them. Notable corporations that have registered include Microsoft and Hewlett Packard.

THE EU MODEL CLAUSES

As we have seen, the Safe Harbor principles only extend to transfers of data between the EU and the USA. The European Commission also released a separate scheme for any transfer out of the EU. A set of what are called 'Model Clauses' enables parties to transfer data outside the EU to other parties located in countries who fall short of the adequate level of protection by means of a private contractual arrangement.

Both parties must execute a fixed prescribed agreement distinct from any other commercial agreement that they may be entering into. Thus, whatever the nature of the commercial deal being struck between film companies in, say, the UK and the USA, the parties must enter into a separate legal agreement which incorporates the prescribed Model Clauses. A good deal of experience has been gained since the Model Clauses were first introduced. For example, a number of business groups such as the International Chambers of Commerce (ICC) and the Confederation of British Industry (CBI) wanted to adapt the clauses to make them more commercially relevant. As a result, in December 2004 the EU issued new Model Clauses to facilitate data flows from the EU. The Model Clauses ensure that data controllers are able to perform data transfers globally under a single set of data protection rules. The new Model Clauses are set out below for reference, but specific legal advice must be taken to establish whether in fact the Clauses apply to the circumstances the film company may operate under. In the specimen Clauses set out we have assumed a transfer of data between a UK film production company, perhaps of its consumer database, to a US-based film distribution company.

It will be appreciated that the issue of transferring data from the UK to any country outside the EU is complex and it is sufficient for the purposes of this book to highlight that a film company wishing to export data must be mindful of the law and take specific legal advice on how to proceed.

SPECIMEN EU MODEL CLAUSES

Standard Contractual Clauses for the Transfer of Personal Data from the Community to Third Countries (controller to controller transfers)

Data Transfer Agreement

Between

Film Production Company Ltd

Whose registered office is at , United Kingdom.

Hereinafter 'data exporter'

And

American Film Distribution Inc

Whose principal place of business is at , California, United States.

Hereinafter 'data importer'

Each a 'party'; together 'the parties'

Definitions

For the purposes of the clauses:

(a) 'Personal data', 'Special categories of data/sensitive data', 'process/ processing', 'controller', 'processor', 'data subject' and 'supervisory authority/authority' shall have the same meaning as in *Directive* 95/46/ EC of 24 October 1995 (whereby 'the authority' shall mean the competent data protection authority in the territory in which the data exporter is established);

(b) the 'data exporter' shall mean the controller who transfers the personal data;

(c) 'the data importer' shall mean the controller who agrees to receive from the data exporter personal data for further processing in accordance with the terms of these clauses and who is not subject to a third country's system ensuring adequate protection;

(d) 'clauses' shall mean these contractual clauses, which are a free-standing document that does not incorporate commercial business terms established by the parties under separate commercial arrangements.

The details of the transfer (as well as the personal data covered) are specified in Appendix B, which forms an integral part of the clauses.

I   Obligations of the data exporter

The data exporter warrants and undertakes that:

(a) The personal data have been collected, processed and transferred in accordance with the laws applicable to the data exporter.

(b) It has used reasonable efforts to determine that the data importer is able to satisfy its legal obligations under these clauses.

(c) It will provide the importer, when so requested, with copies of relevant data protection laws or references to them (where relevant, and not including legal advice) of the country in which the data exporter is established.

(d) It will respond to enquiries from data subjects and the authority concerning processing of the personal data by the data importer, unless the parties have agreed that the data importer will so respond, in which case the data exporter will still respond to the extent reasonably possible and with the information reasonably available to it of the data importer is unwilling or unable to respond. Responses will be made within a reasonable time.

(e) It will make available, upon request, a copy of the clauses to data subjects who are third party beneficiaries under clause III, unless the clauses contain confidential information, in which case it may remove such information. Where information is removed, the data exporter shall inform data subjects in writing of the reason for removal and of their right to draw the removal to the attention of the authority. However, the data exporter shall abide by a decision of the authority regarding access to the full text of the clauses by data subjects, as long as data subjects have agreed to respect the confidentiality of the confidential information removed. The data exporter shall also provide a copy of the clauses to the authority where required.

II   Obligations of the data importer

The data importer warrants and undertakes that:

(a) It will have in place appropriate technical and organisational measures to protect the personal data against accidental or unlawful destruction or accidental loss, alteration, unauthorised disclosure or access, and which provide a level of security appropriate to the risk represented by the processing and the nature of the data to be protected.

(b) It will have in place procedures so that any third party it authorises to have access to the personal data, including processors, will respect and maintain the confidentiality and security of the personal data. Any person acting under the authority of the data importer, including a data processor, shall be obligated to process the personal data only on instructions from the data importer. This provision does not apply to persons authorised or required by law or regulation to have access to the personal data.

(c) It has no reason to believe, at the time of entering into these clauses, in the existence of any local laws that would have a substantial adverse effect on the guarantees provided for under these clauses, and it will inform the data exporter (which will pass such notification on to the authority where required) if it becomes aware of any such laws.

(d) It will process the personal data for purposes described in Annex B, and has the legal authority to give the warranties and fulfil the undertakings set out in these clauses.

(e) It will identify to the data exporter a contact point within its organisation authorised to respond to enquiries concerning processing of the personal data, and it will cooperate in good faith with the data exporter, the data subject and the authority concerning all such enquiries within a reasonable time. In case of legal dissolution of the data exporter, or if the parties have so agreed, the data importer will assume responsibility for compliance with the provisions of clause I(e).

(f) At the request of the data exporter, it will provide the data exporter with evidence of financial resources sufficient to fulfil its responsibilities under the clause III (which may include insurance coverage).

(g) Upon reasonable request of the data exporter, it will submit its data processing facilities, data files and documentation needed for processing to reviewing, auditing and/or certifying by the data exporter (or any independent or impartial inspection agents or auditors, selected by the data exporter and not reasonably objected to by the data importer) to ascertain compliance with the warranties and undertakings in these clauses, with reasonable notice and during regular business hours. The requests will be subject to any necessary consent or approval from a regulatory or supervisory authority within the country of the data importer, which consent or approval the data importer will attempt to obtain in a timely fashion.

(h) It will process the personal data, at its option, in accordance with:

  (i)   the data protection laws of the country in which the data exporter is established, or

  (ii) the relevant provisions of any Commission decision pursuant to Article 25(6) of Directive 95/46/EC, where the data importer complies with the relevant provisions of such an authorisation or decision and is based in a country to which such an authorisation or decision pertains, but is not covered by such authorisation or decision for the purposes of the transfer(s) of the personal data, or

  (iii) the data processing principles set forth in Annex A.

Data importer to indicate which option it selects:_____

Initials of data importer:_____

(j) It will not disclose or transfer the personal data to a third data controller located outside the European Economic Area (EEA) unless it notifies the data exporter about the transfer and

  (i)   the third party data controller processes the personal data in accordance with a Commission decision finding that a third country provides adequate protection, or

  (ii) the third party data controller becomes a signatory to these clauses or another data transfer agreement approved by a competent authority in the EU, or

  (iii) data subjects have been given the opportunity to object, after having been informed of the purposes of the transfer, the categories of recipients and the fact that the countries to which data is exported may have different data protection standards, or

  (iv) with regard to onward transfers of sensitive data, data subjects have given their unambiguous consent to the onward transfer.

III Liability and third party rights

(a) Each party shall be liable to the other parties for damages it causes by any breach of these clauses. Liability as between the parties is limited to actual damage suffered. Punitive damages (ie damages intended to punish a party for its outrageous conduct) are specifically excluded. Each party shall be liable to data subjects for damages it causes by any breach of third party rights under these clauses. This does not affect the liability of the data exporter under its data protection law.

(b) The parties agree that a data subject shall have the right to enforce as a third party beneficiary this clause and clauses I(b), I(d), I(e), II(a), II(c), II(d), II(e), II(h), II(i), III(a), V, VI(d) and VII against the data importer or the data exporter, for their respective breach of their contractual obligations, with regard to his personal data, and accept jurisdiction for this purpose in the data exporter's country of establishment. In cases involving allegations of breach by the data importer, the data subject must first request the data exporter to take appropriate action to enforce his rights against the data importer; if the data exporter does not take such action within a reasonable period (which under normal circumstances would be one month), the data subject may then enforce his rights against the data importer directly. A data subject is entitled to proceed against a data exporter that has failed to use reasonable efforts to determine that the data importer is able to satisfy its legal obligations under these clauses (the data exporter shall have the burden to prove that it took reasonable efforts).

IV Law applicable to the clauses

These clauses shall be governed by the law of the country in which the data exporter is established, with the exception of the laws and regulations relating to processing of the personal data by the data importer under clause II(h), which shall apply only if so selected by the data importer under that clause.

V Resolution of disputes with data subjects or the authority

(a) In the event of a dispute or claim brought by a data subject or the authority concerning the processing of the personal data against either or both of the parties, the parties will inform each other about any such disputes or claims, and will cooperate with a view to settling them amicably in a timely fashion.

(b) The parties agree to respond to any generally available non-binding mediation procedure initiated by a data subject or by the authority. If they do participate in the proceedings, the parties may elect to do so remotely (such as by telephone or other electronic means). The parties also agree to consider participating in any other arbitration, mediation or other dispute resolution proceedings developed for data protection disputes.

(c) Each party shall abide by a decision of a competent court of the data exporter's country of establishment or of the authority which is final and against which no further appeal is possible.

VI Termination

(a) In the event that the data importer is in breach of its obligations under these clauses, then the data exporter may temporarily suspend the transfer of personal data to the data importer until the breach or the contract is terminated.

(b) In the event that:

(i) the transfer of personal data to the data importer has been temporarily suspended by the data exporter for longer than one month pursuant to paragraph (a);

(ii) compliance by the data importer with these clauses would put it in breach of its legal or regulatory obligations in the country of import;

(iii) the data importer is in substantial or persistent breach of any warranties or undertakings given by it under these clauses;

(iv) a final decision against which no further appeal is possible of a competent court of the data exporter's country of establishment or of the authority rules that there has been a breach of the clauses by the data importer or the data exporter; or

(v) a petition is presented for the administration or winding up of the data importer, whether in its personal or business capacity, which petition is not dismissed within the applicable period for such dismissal under applicable law; a winding up order is made; a receiver is appointed over any of its assets; a trustee in bankruptcy is appointed, if the data importer is an individual; a company voluntary arrangement is commenced by it; or any equivalent event in any jurisdiction occurs

then the data exporter, without prejudice ti any other rights it may have against the data importer, shall be entitled to terminate these clauses, in which case the authority shall be informed where required. In cases covered by (i), (ii), or (iv) above the data importer may also terminate these clauses.

(c)   Either party may terminate these clauses if (i) any Commission positive adequacy decision under Article 25(6) of Directive 95/46/EC (or any superceding text) is issued in relation to the country (or a sector thereof) to which the data is transferred and processed by the data importer, or (II) Directive 95/46/EC (or any superceding text) becomes directly applicable in such country.

(d)   The parties agree that the termination of these clauses at any time, in any circumstances and for whatever reason (except for termination under clause VI©) does not exempt them from the obligations and/or conditions under the clauses as regards the processing of the personal data transferred.

VII Variation of these clauses

The parties may not modify these clauses except to update any information in Annex B, in which case they will inform the authority where required. This does not preclude the parties from adding additional commercial clauses where required.

VIII Description of the Transfer

The details of the transfer and of the personal data are specified in Annex B. The parties agree that Annex B may contain confidential business information which they will not disclose to third parties, except as required by law or in response to a competent regulatory or governmental agency, or as required under clause I(e). The parties may execute additional annexes to cover additional transfers, which will be submitted to the authority where required. Annex B may, in the alternative, be drafted to cover multiple transfers.

Dated:_____

American Film Distributor Inc.

FOR DATA IMPORTER

....

....

....

Film Production Company Ltd

FOR DATA EXPORTER

……………………………..

……………………………...

……………………………..

ANNEX A

DATA PROCESSING PRINCIPLES

1. Purpose limitation: Personal data may be processed and subsequently used or further communicated only for purposes described in Annex B or subsequently authorised by the data subject.

2. Data quality and proportionality: Personal data must be accurate and, where necessary, kept up top date. The personal data must be adequate, relevant and not excessive in relation to the purposes for which they are transferred and further processed.

3. Transparency: Data subjects must be provided with information necessary to ensure fair processing (such as information about the purposes of processing and about the transfer), unless such information has already been given by the data exporter.

4. Security and confidentiality: Technical and organisational security measures must be taken by the data controller that are appropriate to the risks, such as against accidental or unlawful destruction or accidental loss, alteration, unauthorised disclosure or access, presented by the processing. Any person acting under the authority of the data controller, including a processor, must not process the data except on instructions from the data controller.

5. Rights of access, rectification, deletion and objection: As provided in Article 12 of Directive 95/46/EC, data subjects must, whether directly or via a third party, be provided with the personal information about them that an organisation holds, except for requests which are manifestly abusive, based on unreasonable intervals or their number or repetitive or systematic nature, or for which access need not be granted under the law of the country of the data exporter. Provided that the authority has given its prior approval, access need also not be granted when doing so

would be likely to seriously harm the interests of the data importer or other organisations dealing with the data importer and such interests are not overridden by the interests for fundamental rights and freedoms of the data subject. The sources of the personal data need not be identified when this is not possible by reasonable efforts, or where the rights of persons other than the individual would be violated. Data subjects must be able to have the personal information about them rectified, amended, or deleted where it is inaccurate or processed against these principles. If there are compelling grounds to doubt the legitimacy of the request, the organisation may require further justifications before proceeding to rectification, amendment or deletion. Notification of any rectification, amendment or deletion to third parties to whom the data have been disclosed need not be made when this involves a disproportionate effort. A data subject must also be able to object to the processing of the personal data relating to him if there are compelling legitimate grounds relating to his particular situation. The burden of proof for any refusal rests on the data importer and the data subject may always challenge a refusal before the authority.

6. Sensitive data: The data importer shall take such additional measures (eg relating to security) as are necessary to protect such sensitive data in accordance with its obligations under clause II.

7. Data used for marketing purposes: Where data are processed for the purposes of direct marketing, effective procedures should exists allowing the data subject at any time to 'opt out' from having his data used for such purposes.

8. Automated decisions: For purposes hereof 'automated decision' shall mean a decision by the data exporter or the data importer which produces legal effects concerning a data subject or significantly affects a data subject and which is based solely on automated processing of personal data intended to evaluate certain personal aspects relating to him, such as his performance at work, creditworthiness, reliability, conduct, etc.The data importer shall not make any automated decisions concerning data subjects except when:

    (a) (i) such decisions are made by the data importer in entering into or performing a contract with the data subject, and

        (ii) (the data subject is given an opportunity to discuss the results of a relevant automated decision with a representative of the parties making such decision or otherwise to make representations to that parties.

Or

(b)   where otherwise provided by the law of the data exporter.

ANNEX B

DESCRIPTION OF THE TRANSFER

(To be completed by the parties)

Data Subjects

The personal data transferred concern the following categories of data subjects:

. . . .

. . . .

Purposes of the transfer(s)

The transfer is made for the following purposes:

. . . .

. . . .

Categories of data

The personal data transferred concern the following categories of data:

. . . .

. . . .

Recipients

The personal data transferred may be disclosed only to the following recipients or categories of recipients:

. . . .

. . . .

Sensitive data (if appropriate)

The personal data transferred concern the following categories of sensitive data:

....

....

Data protection registration information of data exporter (where applicable)

....

....

Additional useful information (storage limits and other relevant information)

....

....

Contact points for data protection enquiries

Data importer   Data exporter

....

....

THE RIGHTS OF INDIVIDUALS AGAINST AN ONLINE FILM BUSINESS

Individuals (or data subjects) have extensive rights under the Act and a film company must comply. The consumer may write to the film company and ask to be supplied with a description, purposes and any disclosures made or a copy of any personal data being held. The film company must respond to that request within 40 days on receipt of a single fee (the fee levels are set by regulations and may alter). The consumer also has the right to prevent processing likely to cause damage. In addition, the consumer has the right to claim compensation from the film company if it contravenes certain requirements of the Act. In the case of inaccurate data, the consumer can apply to the court for correction, blocking, erasure or destruction. Consumers must also be notified when data is being collected and be told how it may be used and who is collecting it.

PENALTIES FOR A FILM COMPANY FOR BREACHING THE DATA PROTECTION ACT

It is a criminal offence not to register where a film company holds appropriate data. A larger threat is that of having to pay compensation where damage has been caused by the loss, unauthorised destruction or disclosure of personal data. There is also, of course, the potential for damaging adverse publicity resulting from such action.

DATABASE RIGHT AND THE FILM COMPANY

We have seen how the rights of individuals are protected by the data protection regime in the EU and what a film company must do to abide by the Data Protection Act. We will now examine what protection the film company has for the database it has sought to compile and concerning which it has gone to great lengths to meet the requirements of the Data Protection Act. Clearly the database that the film company compiles could have enormous commercial value and will likely be the result of considerable effort over a long period of time on the part of that business. We will review the law which governs databases as works which attract financial value.

On 1 January 1998 the *Copyright and Rights in Databases Regulations 1997* ('the Regulations') came into force in this country. The aim was to improve the protection given to databases and harmonise such protection throughout the EU.

A database is defined by Regulation 6 as:

> *a collection of independent works, data or other materials which (a) are arranged in a systematic or methodical way, and b) are individually accessible by electronic or other means.*

The definition captures hard copy databases but it also applies to online collections.

A database right arises automatically, in common with copyright. However, there are two pre-requisites to be met before the right can exist.

In the first place, Regulation 13(1) states that there must have been 'a substantial investment in obtaining, verifying or presenting the contents of the database'. Next, the 'maker' – or if it was compiled jointly, one of its makers – must be a national or, if a company, incorporated in the European Economic Area. The 'maker' is defined by Regulation 14(1) as:

> *the person who takes the initiative in obtaining, verifying or presenting the contents of a database and assumes the risk of investing in that obtaining, verification or presentation.*

It is the maker who will usually be the first owner of the database right. It is important to point out that if the maker is an employee then it is the employer who will be the first owner.

Database right lasts for 15 years from the end of the calendar year in which it was either completed or first made available to the public. It is also possible that a substantial change to the contents of a database will result in this 15 year period commencing again from that time as being considered substantially a new investment. In effect, therefore, it is entirely possible that databases will enjoy a rolling period of protection which could extend for many years beyond first compilation.

Regulation 16 grants the owner the right to prevent the extraction and/or re-utilisation of the whole or a substantial part of the contents of the database. 'Extraction' is defined as the permanent or temporary transfer of any contents of a database to another medium by any means or in any form. 'Re-utilisation' means making those contents available to the public by any means.

As with copyright law there are a number of defences available to the person or company who is alleged to have infringed the database of an owner. These include 'insubstantiality'. This is defined as meaning 'substantial in terms of quantity or quality or a combination of both'. However, it is possible to infringe an owner's database right by a series of what might be insubstantial copying acts. Another defence is that of 'lawful user' in relation to the database. This would include an express licence granted by the owner, or possibly an implied licence. This might be where the owner has not actually given consent for the use of its database but their conduct might lead a court to conclude that the right can be deemed to have granted.

The film company should ensure that the arrangement of its data is systematic or methodical and that the data is individually accessible. In addition, it should maintain a record of the investment it has made in obtaining, verifying or presenting its database. This record must be kept safely. This will be necessary if the film company is ever called upon to prove its investment was 'substantial' and thus attracts the protection of the Regulations. As noted, the continued additions to a database could mean that its period of protection runs well beyond the 15-year right.

PRIVACY POLICIES

It is a requirement that the film company which receives personally identifiable information about its online customers include a privacy policy in its website terms and conditions. We examined the typical provisions one would find in such terms and conditions in Chapter 3. However, it is convenient to detail in this section the broad ambit of the privacy policy the film company would use.

The film company will confirm it is committed to protecting and respecting the privacy of its website visitors and will set out the basis on which any personal data it collects or that is provided to it, will be processed. For the purpose of the Data Protection Act 1998, the data controller will be the film company. It will state that it may collect and process the following data about its visitors: information that they provide by filling in forms on the website. This includes:

1   Information provided at the time of registering to use the website, subscribing to the service, posting material or requesting further services. It will also ask online visitors for information when they enter a competition or promotion sponsored by the film company or when they report a problem with the website. The company will confirm it may keep a record of that correspondence. It may also ask users to complete surveys that it uses for research purposes, although they will be informed they do not have to respond to them.

2   Details of visits to the website including, but not limited to, traffic data, location data, weblogs and other communication data, whether required for the film company's own billing purposes or otherwise, and the resources that its visitors access will be retained by the company and this explained to the user.

The company may collect information about the visitor's computer including, where available, their IP address, operating system and browser type, for system administration and perhaps to report aggregate information to the film company's advertisers (see Chapter 12). This is statistical data about the user's browsing actions and patterns, and does not identify any individual.

For the same reason, the company may obtain information about a visitor's general internet usage by using a cookie file which is stored on the hard drive of the user's computer. The company will explain that cookies enable it:

- to estimate its audience size and usage pattern;

- to store information about visitors' preferences and so allow it to customise its website according to visitors' individual interests;

- to speed up visitors' searches;

- to recognise visitors when they return to the website.

The visitor will be invited to refuse to accept cookies by activating the setting on their browser which allows them to refuse the setting of cookies

The company will explain that unless the visitor has adjusted their browser setting so that it will refuse cookies, the system will issue cookies when the visitor logs on to the website.

The company will state that the data it collects from visitors may be transferred to, and stored at, a destination outside the European Economic Area (EEA). The data may also be processed by staff operating outside the EEA who work for the company or for one of its suppliers. Such staff may be engaged in, among other things, the fulfilment of the online visitor's order, the processing of their payment details and the provision of support services. By supplying their personal data the visitor will be asked to agree to this transfer, storing or processing. The company will confirm that it will take all steps reasonably necessary to ensure that this data is treated securely and in confidence with the privacy policy.

The company should confirm that all information provided to the company by its visitors is stored on its secure servers and that although it does its best to protect personal data, it cannot guarantee the security of such data transmitted to its website.

The way the film company uses the data should be made clear in the privacy policy. For example, the data might be used:

- to ensure that content from its website is presented in the most effective manner for visitors and for their computer;

- to provide visitors with information, products or services that they request from the company or which it feels may interest them, where the visitor has consented to be contacted for such purposes;

- to carry out obligations arising from any contracts entered into between the film company and its online visitors;

- to allow visitors to participate in interactive features of the film company service, when visitors choose to do so;

- to notify visitors about changes to the service.

The film company will state that it may also use data, or permit selected third parties to use data, to provide visitors with information about content, goods and services which may be of interest to the visitor and that the company or the third parties may contact the visitor about these by e-mail, post or telephone.

The policy should explain that if visitors do not want the company to use their data in this way, or to pass details on to third parties for marketing purposes, the visitor must tick the relevant box situated on the online form on which the company collects the data.

The company will explain that it does not disclose information about identifiable individuals to its advertisers, but it might provide them with aggregate information about users. For example, it might inform them that 200 women aged under 30 have clicked on their advertisement on any given day. The company might also use such aggregate information to help advertisers reach the kind of audience they want to target, for example, men in certain post code areas. The film company might make use of the personal data it has collected from visitors to enable it to comply with its advertisers wishes by displaying their advertisement to that target audience.

The film company will explain that it might disclose the personal information of its online visitors to any member of its group, which means its subsidiaries, or ultimate holding company and its subsidiaries, as defined in Section 736 of the UK Companies Act 1985.

Further, it may disclose that personal information to third parties:

- in the event that it sells or buys any business or assets, in which case the film company may disclose the personal data to the prospective seller or buyer of such business or assets;

- if the film company or substantially all of its assets are acquired by a third party, in which case personal data held by it about its customers will be one of the transferred assets;

- if the film company is under a duty to disclose or share the visitors personal data in order to comply with any legal obligation, or to protect the rights, property, or safety of the company, its customers, or others. This might include exchanging information with other companies and organisations for the purposes of fraud protection and credit risk reduction.

The rights of the film company's online visitors will be set out in the privacy policy. For example, they will have the right to ask the company not to process personal data for marketing purposes. The company will say that it usually informs visitors (before collecting their data) if it intends to use their data for such purposes or if it intends to disclose that information to any third party for such purposes. The visitor will be told they can exercise their right to prevent such processing by checking certain boxes on the forms the company uses to collect such data.

The company will state that its website might, from time to time, contain links to and from the websites of its partner networks, advertisers and affiliates. If the visitor follows a link to any of those websites, it will be made clear that those websites have their own privacy policies and that the company does not accept any responsibility or liability for those policies. The visitor will be advised to check these policies before they submit any personal data to such websites.

The Data Protection Act 1998 gives individuals the right to access information held about them. Thus, the film company will confirm that the visitor's right of access can be exercised in accordance with the Act. Any access request may be subject to a fee, for example £10, to meet the costs in providing visitors with details of the information held about them.

CHECKLIST

- Ensure that the film company is registered under the Data Protection Act 1998 if the website is collecting personal information about individual visitors.

- The film website must display a full privacy policy and the website legal terms and conditions must contain full information about the individual's rights in relation to their personal data.

- Ensure that the film company understands the eight data protection principles under the Data Protection Act 1998.

- If the film company will be transferring personal data outside the European Union then it must use the Model Clauses or sign up to the US Safe Harbor if the transfer is to the USA.

CHAPTER 8

The Distance Selling Regulations and Online Film and Merchandise Sales

BACKGROUND

The sale of film DVDs by retailers over the internet is now commonplace. Items of this kind are low risk in the eyes of the purchaser in that they are probably already aware of the product and its content and the modest value of the unit means they are more willing to consider an online purchase. Other physical merchandise which might be offered for sale online by a film company may similarly be of slight consequence, or the item may be more difficult for the consumer to assess until they actually receive the goods. In any event, there is a good deal of scope for a film company to make products available by means of the internet. These products can be distributed to a worldwide audience, if desired, and with modern logistics most can be dispatched and delivered to the consumer within a matter of days anywhere across the globe.

However, there are important legal considerations of which a film company must be aware before offering merchandise for sale via the internet. These rules only apply to businesses based within the European Union where that business supplies to an online purchaser. The laws we are about to consider do not apply where merchandise is sold online to other businesses.

The background to the consumer protection legislation that forms the subject of this chapter lies in the EU's desire to protect consumers who enter into contracts for the purchase of goods or services away from business premises. It was considered that people should have the opportunity to examine the goods or services being offered as they would have done if buying in a shop. Thus, a cooling-off period would be desirable. The legislative tool by which contracts concluded at a distance are governed is the Consumer Protection (Contracts Concluded by Means of Distance Selling) Regulations 2000. Despite the date of the Regulations they were, in fact, not written with the internet in mind, although by definition an internet sale is a distance contract. They therefore apply to online sales of goods and services by businesses based in the EU to consumers similarly based anywhere in the EU. The Regulations are commonly referred to as the 'Distance Selling Regulations'.

THE CONSUMER PROTECTION (CONTRACTS CONCLUDED BY MEANS OF DISTANCE COMMUNICATION) REGULATIONS 2000

The *Distance Selling Directive* was adopted by the European Parliament and Council in May 1997 and has been implemented by the UK by the *Consumer Protection (Contracts Concluded by Means of Distance Communication) Regulation 2000 (SI 2000 No. 2334)* (the Regulations).

The Regulations came into force in this country on 31 October 2000. However, on 6 April 2005 the Consumer Protection (Distance Selling) (Amendments) Regulations 2005 also came into force. These change the original Regulations in relation to certain issues.

THE AIM OF THE REGULATIONS

The Distance Selling Regulations give consumers certain rights and protection when they shop for goods or services 'at a distance'. The purpose of the legislation is to:

- give consumers confidence in purchasing goods and/or services where there is no face-to-face contact with the seller;

- ensure that all traders operating distance selling schemes meet certain basic requirements.

In brief, the Distance Selling Regulations say that you must always give your customers certain clear information. This is so that they have the information they need to decide whether to buy from you. In most cases you must also give customers the right to a cancellation period.

The information you must give include details about comprises:

- your business;

- your goods or services;

- your payment arrangements;

- your delivery arrangements;

- your customers' right to cancel their orders.

THE DEFINITION OF A 'DISTANCE CONTRACT'

Distance Contracts are defined broadly as:

Any contract concerning goods or services concluded between a supplier and a consumer under an organised distance sales or service provision scheme run by the supplier, who, for the purpose of the contract, makes exclusive use of one or means of distance communication up to and including the moment at which the contract is concluded.

The key to the applicability of the Regulations is a contract where the supplier and the consumer do not come face-to-face prior to the conclusion of the contract. They provide protection for consumers in the UK shopping for goods and services by telephone, mail order, fax, interactive TV and the internet.

The Regulations harmonise laws in all member states so that all European consumers have equality of access to goods and services in other member states.

INFORMATION TO BE PROVIDED BY A FILM COMPANY TO ITS ONLINE AUDIENCE UNDER THE REGULATIONS

The Regulations specify that, prior to the conclusion of any distance contract, a consumer must be provided with certain information. The film company is required to provide such information clearly and comprehensibly in good time before the internet sale is made. This detail should be included on the film company's website and includes the following information:

1   the film company's identity: if the contract requires payment in advance, the company's address should be displayed on the website. We have seen in Chapter 4 that, in any event, under the E-Commerce Regulations 2002, a film company which sells merchandise or services via its website must provide this detail;

2   the principle characteristics of the company's goods or services;

3   all prices including taxes;

4   details of how payment can be made;

5   the length of time the price or any special offers remain valid

6   the minimum duration of the contract in the case of contracts for the supply of goods or services to be provided either permanently or recurrently;

7   delivery costs, as well as all payment arrangements;

8   whether it proposes to supply substitute merchandise or services of equivalent quality and price in the event of merchandise or services ordered by the consumer being unavailable;

9   the right of the online consumer to cancel;

10   where customers are to use a premium rate telephone number, the cost of the call must be specified before charges are incurred for the telephone call;

11   any costs of using the internet as a means of distance communication must be highlighted.

All the above information can be supplied by the film company to the consumer by e-mail.

CARRYING OUT THE CONTRACT

Any contract for the delivery of merchandise to the customer must be carried out within the time limits agreed with the customer as stated in the website terms and conditions. If no period has been agreed, the statutory time limit is within a maximum of 30 days from the day after the day the customer sends the order to the film company.

If the film company is unable to meet the deadline, it must inform the customer before the expiry of the deadline and refund any money paid in relation to the contract. The refund should be made as quickly as possible and certainly within 30 days, including weekends and public holidays. It is open to the company and the customer to agree a revised date for delivery of the merchandise. The customer, however, is not under an obligation to agree a revised date. If the customer does not agree to a revised date the contract must be treated as if it had not been made. Any money paid in relation to the contract must be returned to the customer as quickly as possible and certainly within 30 days from the date of cancellation.

CANCELLING ORDERS WITH THE FILM COMPANY

Provided the film company gives its customer the required written information at the latest at the time the merchandise is delivered, cancellation rights end seven working days after the day on which the goods have been received.

If the company does not give its customer the required information at the latest at the time the merchandise is delivered, but does so within three months from the day after the day customer receives the merchandise, then the customer's cancellation rights will end after the day on which the customer received the required written information.

Where the company has not provided the required written information, the customer's cancellation rights will end after the three months and seven working days counting the day after the customer received the merchandise.

CONTRACTS WHICH FALL OUTSIDE THE CONSUMER PROTECTION (CONTRACTS CONCLUDED BY MEANS OF DISTANCE COMMUNICATION) REGULATIONS 2000

Certain contracts are excluded from the operation of the Regulations. These include contracts for the supply of foodstuffs, beverages or other goods intended for everyday consumption supplied to the home of the consumer, to his or her residence, or to his or her workplace. Thus, internet sales of, perhaps, film title branded foodstuffs such as sweets will not be subject to the Regulations because of the perishable nature of the goods concerned. Audio or video recordings or computer software which the film company consumer has 'unsealed' are excluded.

In addition, contracts for the provision of accommodation, transport, catering or leisure services, where the supplier undertakes when the contract is concluded to provide these services on a specific date or within a specific period, for example, hotel and travel bookings are not covered by the Regulations. Thus, if the film company makes available via its website a facility for audiences to make bookings for cinema tickets combined with travel and overnight hotel stay, such an offer will not fall under the Regulations.

Other exceptions to the general right to withdraw include contracts are:

a) for the provision of services if performance has begun, with the consumer's agreement, before the end of seven working days;

b) for the supply of goods or services, the price of which is dependent on fluctuations in financial markets that cannot be controlled by the film company;

c) for the supply of goods made to the consumer's specifications or personalised or which, by reason of their nature, cannot be returned or are liable to deteriorate or expire rapidly. For example, a film retailer might make an exclusive offer via its website to the first thousand visitors to the website for a personalised item of merchandise. Such merchandise falls outside the scope of the Regulations;

d)   for the supply of newspapers, periodicals and magazines;

e)   for gaming and lottery services.

The question arises of whether the provision of a link on a website operated by the film company from where customers, on payment, can download a film or music, or from where customers can buy ringtones and screensavers for mobile phones, for example, by texting or telephoning a particular number, falls within the cancellation exemptions referred to above. The answer is that in such cases the consumer is not receiving a physical good as such. If the supply is therefore not of an actual good but rather of a service, the exception to the right to cancel would only apply if the film company has the customer's agreement to start the service before the end of the cancellation period and the company has provided the customer with the required written information before it starts the service, including information that their cancellation rights will end as soon as the service begins.

Another issue in interpretation of the Regulations is whether the exceptions above apply to products which may be the subject of copyright, for example, books or, of course, film. The answer appears to be no. Copyright considerations might underlie the partial exceptions provided in the Regulations for the supply of audio, video/DVD recordings or computer software that the consumer has unsealed. However, there is no general exception for copyright products and the exception probably would not extend to other products that may lend themselves to copying such as books, perhaps about the film title production, or sheet music to the soundtrack. Nevertheless, this does not stop the film company from specifying in its website terms and conditions what it considers to be reasonable care in customers examining such goods. However, if the customer has done no more than examine the goods as they would have in a shop and if that requires opening the packaging and trying out the goods, then they would not have breached their duty to take reasonable care of the goods. In a shop books and sheet music are usually displayed unsealed.

A review of the exceptions listed above should enable a film company to establish whether the services they offer online fall outside the Regulations and thus do not allow their online customers to withdraw from the contract. It is important to note that full treatment must be given on the matter of cancellation rights in the film company's website terms and conditions and that legal advice should be taken as to the contents of those terms and conditions as they will cover items not capable of comprehensive review in this book.

THE CONSUMER PROTECTION (DISTANCE SELLING) (AMENDMENTS) REGULATIONS 2005

The principal aim of the changes to the Distance Selling Regulations is to make the right of cancellation clearer in the context of the provision of services. Prior to the amendments there was a requirement on a business to inform the consumer in writing or another durable medium before the contract is made that he or she will not be able to cancel the contract once performance of the services has begun with his or her agreement. This created problems for some businesses that receive orders over the phone for services which consumers want straight away or within a few days. In such cases compliance with the Regulations was impracticable or unduly costly if information needed to be faxed or sent urgently by post or even courier. It also meant that performance of the services could well be delayed.

To overcome these problems the right to cancel has been amended. For a film company, the new provisions could be important to understand where the business is offering some form of service and this service is available to consumers not only via the website but perhaps by telephone request. This is most likely to arise through the use of mobile phones, where the film consumer is required to call in to take advantage of an offer of services and the contract is effectively concluded via that phone call. We will therefore now examine the effect of the changes in that context.

The film company is no longer required to inform the consumer prior to the conclusion of a contract for services that he or she will not be able to cancel once performance has begun with his or her agreement. Under the changed provision, the film company must, in such cases, provide the consumer with information as to how the right to cancel may be affected if the consumer agrees to the performance beginning fewer than seven working days after the contract was concluded. This information must be provided prior to or in good time during the performance of the contract.

Next, where the film company providing services gives information as to how the right to cancel may be affected as set out above before performance of those services begins and the consumer agrees to such performance beginning before the end of the cooling-off period, there is no right to cancel.

Where the film company providing services gives information as to how the right to cancel may be affected as set out above in good time during the performance of the services, there is a right to cancel even if the consumer agrees to performance beginning within the seven working days of the contract being concluded, but the cooling-off period begins when the consumer receives the information and ends seven working days later or when performance is completed (whichever is sooner).

The film company can still exclude the right to cancel by including terms in their contracts with consumers to the effect that the consumer agrees that the services will begin before the end of the cooling-off period. In order to do this, the film company will need to inform consumers about the loss of the right to cancel prior to the contract being concluded unless agreement is sought from the consumer otherwise than as part of the contract.

Where, however, the film company is happy not to exclude the right to cancel, information concerning the right to cancel can be provided in good time during the performance of the services rather than prior to the conclusion of the contract.

The consumer's right to cancel is lost when the performance of the services is completed. This may prove difficult though where there is not 'good time' to provide information about the cancellation right before the services are completed. Where the information is not provided in good time but the services have been substantially performed or are completed, the right of cancellation is preserved.

GUIDANCE FOR THE DISTANCE SELLING REGULATIONS

The Office of Fair Trading and the Department of Trade and Industry have issued joint guidance that will update and inform those selling online of their duties under the Distance Selling Regulations. The guidance seeks to clarify some ambiguities after the Regulations came into force. It is felt there are still some areas of confusion.

It is clear what the online film company must do on the matter of refunds for the supply of, for example, DVDs or other merchandise. If a customer cancels an order for merchandise by e-mail but fails to return the item, the film company cannot delay making the refund. The refund must be made as soon as possible after the customer cancels and within 30 days at the latest. Interestingly, even if the consumer returns merchandise which is damaged they still do not lose their right to cancel under the Regulations. Clearly the film company still has a right of action against its online customer for failing to take reasonable care of the merchandise, but this could prove difficult and on occasion hardly worth the time and money involved in the effort.

There is also the question of how much the refund to the online customer should be. If the film company supplies merchandise such as title promotional clothes, the full price paid for the clothes, including the cost of delivery, must be refunded. However, what if the film company also offers other services such as gift wrapping or express delivery of the item? It is recommended that the film company service should be structured so that there is one contract for the supply of goods, where a refund is available, and another for a supply of services, which is non-refundable.

CHECKLIST

- If the film company is selling physical merchandise online to consumers in the EU then the Distance Selling Regulations apply.

- Certain products and services are excluded from the Regulations, including foodstuffs and online hotel or flight bookings.

CHAPTER 9

Paying for Film Downloads

INTRODUCTION

Most transactions conducted over the internet at present use existing payment products such as credit cards. However, as online commerce grows, new easy methods of payment are being introduced. In large part these are targeted at products which may be fashionable and whose appeal lies in immediacy of access.

The primary concern with all payments made online has been one of security. Whilst more people than ever are comfortable with the internet and with buying items online using their credit cards, the fact remains that fear of fraud remains a significant barrier to e-commerce.

In this section we will consider the relationship between the internet and the laws of money.

ELECTRONIC PAYMENT SYSTEMS

The fact that electronic payments to acquire merchandise or services over the internet involve electronic transfers is, of course, not unique. Most retailers employ debit card transactions which are also electronic transactions.

The inertia which acts on adoption of electronic payment over the internet is not merely predicated upon concerns over the security of the transaction between payer and payee. The identity of the payer and irrevocability of the payment are also factors, as is universal acceptance of the type of electronic payment.

CREDIT CARDS

Most business-to-consumer transactions conducted online are effected by credit card payments. The purchaser inserts their credit card details by completing an online form which is then transmitted to the seller over the internet. The transmission is usually encrypted, which provides additional security.

Film companies find this most common of payment methods attractive for a number of reasons. From the consumer's point of view, credit cards are familiar. They need not enter into additional agreements and there are no currency conversion problems. Moreover, the consumer buying online using their credit card has the protection of the Consumer Credit Act 1974, placing them in a better position than if they pay in cash. For example, Section 75 of the Consumer Credit Act applies to transactions where any single item is worth between £100 and £30,000. If there is no pre-existing agreement between the card issuer and the supplier, the cardholder has enhanced legal rights. They can pursue either the supplier or the card issuer itself for misrepresentation or breach of contract. This is because the Act makes the card supplier jointly and severally liable. From the perspective of the film company selling merchandise or services, using credit cards also has advantages. There is no need for specialist equipment to be installed by potential customers and thus purchasing online is easier for internet users.

The principal disadvantage to the film company as a vendor is the need for it to enter into a merchant account with a card issuer. This is necessary to allow the business to accept credit cards. Another factor to consider is the transactions costs associated with credit card payments.

Internet card payment transactions are classed as 'card not present' (CNP) transactions. As the cardholder (and the card) are not physically with the online film company at the time of the transaction, it is not possible for the company to check details or the customer's signature.

There are risks associated with CNP transactions which the film company must understand and make a commercial judgement on. Primarily, whenever the business concludes an internet transaction there is no guarantee of payment. If the online customer should query the transaction at a later date or any discrepancies arise, the card issuer might resort to a charge back to recover funds from the film company. Unfortunately, fraud is common where the cardholder is not present.

The film company might encounter a number of problems in the context of CNP transactions. The customer might claim that the card was used fraudulently or deny the transaction. They might maintain that the card has been stolen or claim that the card number has been used without their authority. Finally, they might say that they never received the merchandise or argue that it is defective, not as described or not of merchantable quality. In each of these cases a charge back may result. It is therefore very important that the film company encourages its staff to record details accurately and to be vigilant.

The company should always keep a record of the details of the transaction. This is because it may need to provide the credit card merchant with such details if the online customer subsequently queries the transaction with their card company. The customer might query the date of transaction or their card number. The film company should retain records for at least three years.

There exists a tripartite relationship between the film company, the card issuer and the online customer. In the UK case law has established that using a credit card creates three distinct legal contracts. The first is the contract of supply between the film company and its cardholding online customer. Second is the contract between the film company and the card-issuing company. The card issuer undertakes to honour the card by paying the film company upon presentation of the sales voucher. Third, there is the contract between the card-issuing company and the internet customer. The cardholding customer undertakes to reimburse the card issuer for all payments made or liabilities incurred by the card issuer to the film company as a result of the customer's use of their credit card. It can be seen that in each contract, each party is involved in two of the three contracts but none is party to all three.

A cardholder who purchases by credit card completes that contract with the film company as supplier of the merchandise or services. The film company must then look to the card issuer for payment. The effect is that, if the card issuer fails to pay the film company – for example, if the issuer becomes insolvent – the film company cannot then seek payment from its online customer.

The most significant risk to the film company that adopts a credit card facility is one which pertains to any retailer who subscribes to a credit card merchant agreement. Section 83 of the Consumer Credit Act 1974 states that generally a consumer cannot be made liable for the misuse of his or her credit card by a third party. Usually, the credit card agreement makes the cardholder liable for the first £50 while the card is not in their possession until the card issuer receives notification of the card's loss.

Nonetheless, the internet customer using their card can, within a certain time limit, dispute a transaction that may be the result of theft, fraud or error. If the card issuer accepts that payment should not proceed a 'charge back' occurs. The film company might not only have to repay the disputed sums but also a processing fee. Given that on any one transaction the majority of internet purchases are for modest values such as film downloads, the processing fee might exceed the transaction value.

As all transactions that the film company completes online will be conducted in this way, it might prove more difficult for the business to obtain a merchant account. The card issuer will usually require the film company to provide additional eligibility information. This might mean the film company having to disclose to the card issuer its volume of business, credit history, cost of merchandise, debt load, length of time in business and refund policies.

In addition, if the product or services can actually be delivered electronically, they can be denied more easily. Where physical merchandise is supplied, the film company can usually prove that the goods have been delivered to its customer's address. The internet customer cannot therefore argue that the transaction did not take place. They can probably only allege that the merchandise was not what they ordered or is defective. So it can be seen that, if the film company is delivering online, while the cost of reproducing and delivering the merchandise might be lower it might suffer the payment of numerous charge backs with attendant processing fees. If this were multiplied, the film company might even lose its merchant account.

SECURE ELECTRONIC TRANSACTIONS (SET)

The 'Secure Electronic Payment Protocol' is based on encryption technology. Its aim is to provide an agreed security standard for use in making payments over the internet. It was intended to maintain the privacy of internet transactions. In addition, it addresses the needs for the identity of the payer to be verified so that his or her instructions can be relied upon.

Secure Electronic Transactions work as follows. Two separate keys, one public and one private, are used to encode and decode the message. The public key encrypts the message using a complex formula. The message is then transmitted over the internet in an encrypted form. The public key is published in a directory and therefore can be assessed by third parties. However, the message sent can only be read using the private key, and this will only be known to the receiver.

The identity of the sender is established by the use of digital certificates. These verify that the film company concerned has the authority to use the public key in which the message sent is encrypted. The certificates are in the form of small electronic documents issued by Certification Authorities. The use of these certificates is coupled with the use of a digital signature which operates by encrypting the message in a cryptographic algorithm called a hash function. The encryption is made using the sender's private key. The sender's public key is then used by a recipient to reconstitute the hash and is compared with other hashes generated by the sender for authenticity. This process of authenticating identity is rather like checking a handwritten signature on a cheque against a cheque card.

It is important for the film company to ensure non-repudiation by the sender. A traditional payment method such as a cheque can be cancelled at any point before it is cashed. The only way to achieve irrevocability with online payment is to take one further step. It is necessary for the film company to incorporate into its website terms and conditions an express stipulation that any instructions/payments are irrevocable once sent unless proved not to be authentic.

MICRO PAYMENT SYSTEMS

The internet is the perfect medium for accessing low cost items which can be downloaded easily and for which transaction values often do not exceed more than a few pounds. Many of these are directed towards the youth market. Examples in the film industry include film video downloads, screensavers and SMS bulletins with the latest news about title releases. Such transactions have a huge effect on e-commerce and are highly successful. However, they do not warrant the use of credit cards and their attraction is the immediacy of their offer. To meet the demand for such items a new form of online payment geared towards low cost purchases has developed. It is known as micro payment.

One example in the UK is the telecommunications giant BT's *Click & Buy Service*. This system permits the user to buy online items or services which might involve modest sums. The total is then added at the end of the month to the user's fixed telephone bill, which records all transactions made online whereby the user's account was operated. Micro payment systems are a breakthrough as they overcome the security concerns that exist with online payment. In addition, they permit those under 16 to make purchases over the internet and via mobile phones against a pre-determined monthly amount set by the parent.

We will now briefly examine the typical provisions found in a contract between a film company wishing to offer, for example, film videos for viewing on mobile phones and the micro payment service provider company.

TYPICAL PROVISIONS IN MICRO PAYMENT CONTRACTS

It is almost certain to be the case that the film company will have to operate on the basis of the standard terms and conditions which the micro payment provider issues. The film company will not have any scope for revision of those terms.

The business model we will examine consists of the micro payment service provider, the film company wishing to provide content such as film downloads to its online consumers and finally the online consumer who wishes to buy that content and therefore use the micro payment system. In the BT Click & Buy arrangement, the consumer has an account and the value of the items purchased online in any month is added to the consumer's standard phone bill. It is a simple process but one which permits lower value internet transactions for items where use of a credit card would be a barrier to the sale.

The micro payment provider will charge the film company a percentage fee on each transaction completed using the service. It will also probably charge an upfront integration fee for setting up the micro payment system and integrating it with the film company's website.

The service provider company, who we shall refer to as Micro, will confirm in the Agreement that it will provide the micro payment service to the film company with the reasonable skill and care of a competent provider of such services.

In order to set up the service Micro will need to integrate its system with the website operated by the film company. The Agreement will make clear that, before the service is provided, a detailed process must be followed to establish and test the system integration between Micro and film company. In any event Micro will not offer any warranties that its system will be free from faults and the film company will be required to accept that failures of the service may occur from time to time.

Micro will usually state that there can be no guarantee of security on the internet and therefore it will not warrant that it will be able to keep the film company's transactions secure.

It will be necessary for the micro payment service to be maintained at various intervals and Micro will make clear that for operational reasons it may change the technical specification of its service or suspend it for maintenance or because of an emergency. In each case Micro will endeavour to give as much notice as possible to the film company.

The consumer who buys the film company's merchandise using the micro payment service will be billed per transaction and, whatever the basis of that charge including value and when levied, that will be set out in the agreement between the film company and Micro. Any changes or additions to that basis must be managed by the film company as directed by Micro.

The whole payment process must be reported accurately and this will be typically be done by Micro providing the film company with information on a monthly basis in the form of a Statement of Account. This will detail the value of all online sales during the previous month, include an invoice from Micro to the film company showing Micro's charges and any sales which Micro has been unable to collect from the consumer. Micro will withhold or recover monies paid to the film company if the consumer does not pay for the online items or, for example, if the sum paid is duplicated in error. It may be that Micro will include a provision in its contract with the film company allowing it to charge a retainer on a percentage basis each month. This retention will cover anticipated non-payments by a film company's consumer and will be reviewed perhaps quarterly to ensure the retention is based on actual levels of non-payment over such period.

The Agreement will place the obligation of security for passwords and usernames which the film company adopts for access to its website on the film company itself. Micro may include a right to suspend its service if it believes that a breach of security has occurred.

No offensive or indecent material should be offered by the film company via its website by use of the micro payment system and Micro will reserve the right to terminate the service in such circumstances.

The intellectual property rights in the software which supports the micro payment service will be expressly reserved in favour of Micro or its licensors if in fact Micro has itself taken a licence for the software from a third party provider.

The circumstances under which the Agreement between Micro and the film company can be terminated will be set out, whether for reasons of breach or if the commercial relationship is to come to an end for simple business operational reasons. In the event of termination Micro will call for the return of any material, including hardware, software and documentation that it has provided to the film company in support of the service.

It can be seen that there are many issues to cover in a relationship between the film company and the micro payment service provider. Our review is illustrative, but full legal advice must be sought if such a strategic relationship is being considered.

CHECKLIST

- Explore the various payment facilities now available for internet sales. If likely to be providing products or services with modest prices, consider micro payment services.

- Examine the cost implications on entering into a micro payment facility with a provider.

CHAPTER 10

Engaging with New Content Platforms

BACKGROUND

There is rapid convergence of audiovisual media, broadband networks and electronic devices. The demand is for rich media content on any screen, anywhere. The availability and take up of high speed broadband connections is making it easier for consumers not only to access a wider range of creative digital content than would have been imaginable 10 years ago, but also to create content themselves. At the same time, broadband's ability to handle vast quantities of data enables film companies to offer new content and services and to create additional markets.

It is important for the film company to understand how it can engage with the new breed of telecommunication companies, Internet Service Providers, mobile platforms and content aggregators to open up new channels for film distribution. These gatekeepers to the market are looking for new ways to retain and increase market share. Film and television content is the answer. In essence, the mobile phone operators need content they can package in different forms. They require film companies to concentrate on what they do best, which is creating content, capturing people's imaginations and storytelling. There is a demand for more made-for-mobile content. That might include a combination of highlights and tasters for programmes but also mobile versions of shows. The mobile operators, for their part, can concentrate on delivering the best possible experience of that content to mutual customers. They can tailor the content for different formats using their knowledge of the customer. At this stage of the development of new media, content owners and content aggregators are engaged in a period of experimentation, since there is not yet a perfect model. The content owner needs to ensure that they do not jeopardise their existing relationships with established platforms but at the same time yield financial reward in the new media environment. They must strike this balance in the absence of hard data about the actual levels of migration by viewers from linear to on-demand services. Whatever commercial model the film company seeks to implement with the content aggregator, there will be several issues to understand.

The issues will be manifold, including what financing models can these new gatekeepers provide? Who does the film company need to go to and how does it need to deal with them? What are the rights opportunities around for example broadband video-on-demand?

These matters require careful consideration and, once strategic partners have been identified by the film company, properly drafted legal agreements need to be implemented. We will now consider some of those agreements.

FILM AND TELEVISION WEBSITE DESIGN AND DEVELOPMENT AGREEMENT

It is clear that the vital relationship to the online activity of a film company is the relationship with its website designer or developer. In the early years of e-commerce few businesses that elected to operate online gave much thought to the key terms they should have with their website designers. The industry was new and many website development firms had not grown from other businesses and thus, on both sides of the arrangement, potential problems could not be appreciated.

As the industry matured and experience was gained on the part of those instructing website developers, problems began to be apparent. These tended to be issues around what happened when the website designer's services were to be dispensed with. There were disputes over ownership of intellectual property rights in the website, domain name transfer and hosting of the website. Some 10 years on these issues remain of vital significance, but most website developers work to standard contracts with their clients and the majority of clients now expect to sign such an agreement and are clearer as to what they wish to see in the contractual relationship.

It should be appreciated that the media world and the software development world are very different environments and each consists of professionals who may not be hugely experienced in online film and television distribution. There are, of course, many new media agencies who cross over from pure website software developers to more media agency, and they have an excellent understanding of online techniques. This will have been obtained from experience over a number of years with sectors other than the film industry. Therefore they might need to grasp the needs of the film and broadcast sectors quickly. At the same time the film company might be inexperienced in offering their catalogue over the internet either as a download-to-own service or perhaps by selling their title DVDs online. The potential for misunderstanding in the relationship is thus significant. In addition, whilst many new media agencies and website developers will present their standard terms to the film company it is important to state that these should always be capable of being amended to reflect the commercial imperatives of the film company. Careful legal advice needs to be obtained on the negotiation of this relationship and the Agreement which records its terms.

For a film company there are some key issues to consider in the contract to be entered into with its website design and development company. In this section we will examine those matters from the perspective of the film company as opposed to the website design company. It is important to emphasise this as there is a number of issues where the designer and the film company will have different commercial expectations. It will often be a question of negotiation as to what forms the final contract. We will review those matters that the film company would find desirable.

The designer will be appointed on the basis of the terms and conditions in the Film or Television Website Design and Development Agreement ('the Agreement'). The designer will be required to design the website in accordance with an agreed specification and an agreed time period. This question of the specification is a frequent source of dispute. On occasion the film company might require certain functionality of the website but might not communicate its aims sufficiently clearly to the website designer. The full functionality of the website must be clearly spelled out and the place to do this is in the technical specification. The specification usually forms a schedule to the Agreement as this is the part which will change for each website produced by the designer, whereas the contractual terms may well remain substantially the same from deal to deal. It is important to note that agreements of this kind can be technically complex from both a legal and an IT perspective. The film company must approach the relationship with very clear business and technological objectives. Both issues will determine the content of the Agreement. The film company must ensure that it understands the required format and functionality of the website precisely. Sometimes the lawyers will not be able to comment to any significant degree on the technical specification for the website and might assume that the film company client does. As has been stated, the worlds of software and media are not the same and therefore the film company must spend time with the developer in understanding what is meant by certain technical terms.

The Agreement will cover the fees which are to be paid by the film company for its website. It is not uncommon for those fees, once agreed, to be met over various intervals of the design process. For example, a certain percentage will be paid on signing the Agreement, further payments to be made on presentation of the 'look and feel' stage of the design, or at other testing phases, and the remaining sum a week after live running of the website once online.

Clearly the music business will want to retain as much control over the content of its website as possible and this impacts on the question of intellectual property rights. To enable the development of the website the music business will provide the designer with a good deal of material including, of course, the film content itself, DVD cover or poster text, photographs, video images, logos, trade names and so on. The intellectual property rights in those materials will almost certainly belong to the film company or a third party. Therefore the intellectual property rights in that content will reside with the film company or be otherwise licensed to it by the third party. They will not belong to the website designer. The form of that intellectual property might be copyright in the film work, text or photographs and perhaps trademarks in the name of the business, or certain titles or services it provides.

However, the website designer is being asked to design a website and the functionality of the website and the underlying software code may well be the result of original work by the designer, which in itself attracts copyright. Website designers will usually only grant a licence for these rights to their clients but will retain ownership. This is because those rights represent the value to the designer in its enterprise. There are circumstances where the film company will want to expressly acquire the intellectual property rights in its entire website. If the contract between the two is silent on the point, the designer would be deemed to own the rights in the software as original author. If the film company does wish to hold the rights, therefore, this must be made clear in the Agreement. Typically the designer would charge a premium for the release of the rights to the film company.

The film company would wish to approve all content in its website before the website goes live on the worldwide web and this right should be stated in the Agreement. One issue which is not uncommon between the parties is the constant shifting of requirements, usually on the part of the web designer's client. This can lead to friction at the very least. The opportunity for the designer to get the film company to approve content at certain specified stages in the website development is important as, once passed, the Agreement will usually state that no further changes may be made by the film company unless these fall outside the scope of the original work. This will inevitably involve further fees.

If the film company decides to make changes to its proposed website during the design process or after completion of the website, then the Agreement should specify a clear process to follow. This issue is actually quite significant, given the dynamic nature of website design and the competitive nature of the film and television industries. It is possible for a film company to discover that an innovative service is being offered by a competitor online and wish to make rapid changes to its own website to capture the new market. Any further costs associated with the changes requested by the film company would be notified to the film company first under the terms of the change request procedure.

In most instances the film company will simply assume that the designer has appropriate personnel equal to the task of developing its website. However, it is a good idea to include a provision confirming that the designer will at all times have sufficient personnel to perform their contractual obligations under the Agreement. This can be a somewhat nebulous issue, though. There are no recognised standards in terms of skills of new media agencies – they are usually either good or not so good. Nonetheless, it is as well to include a provision of this kind in any event.

It is common for staff in web design companies to move to other companies in the industry and often those staff are key in terms of their particular skills in certain aspects of web design or indeed the ongoing relationship between the film company and the website design agency. It is important to emphasise that – such is the significance of new media platforms – the service provided by a film company is likely to be ongoing and constantly evolving. The film company might simply engage the website designer to act on retainer and introduce and implement new ideas in the new media sphere as they become apparent to ensure the film company retains market advantage. A film company could find itself facing a delay in construction of its website or, worse, the inability of the designer to complete certain desired features of the website in the absence of appropriate personnel. The Agreement should include a clause giving the film company the right to terminate the Agreement if this situation occurs.

As stated, most web design work is undertaken in stages and there are testing intervals which serve as useful opportunities to review progress and performance of the website designer. The Agreement should contain provisions which allow the film company to terminate the contract if at those stages the work is not satisfactory. However, the right to terminate would only arise following an agreed notification process to enable the designer to respond to any legitimate concerns the film company might have over the construction process.

The period for which the Agreement is to run must be stated. This can be for a fixed term – for example, one year – and then run on a rolling basis until terminated by either party. This is more usual where the designer is to provide ongoing services to the film company such as consultancy support or training for the website. There must also be express provisions in the Agreement dealing with the circumstances in which the Agreement can be terminated early. This usually revolves around a significant breach by one of the parties of its obligations under the Agreement. A standard clause would also see an ability to terminate if the other party becomes insolvent.

The consequences of termination must be made clear. If the website designer is in breach the film company will want to be able to recover material supplied to the designer or material which is central to the successful operation of the website. This might include all software documentation to enable a third party designer appointed by the film company to load onto another server and ensure continuity of the film company's service.

There is always a need to maintain confidentiality with regard to each party's business. During the development phase, and even thereafter as long as there is commercial dialogue between the designer and film company, certain information will be revealed which is by its nature confidential. The film company might well be seeking to launch a new service to promote an artist which must be kept secret until the website is launched or that service promoted via the website. In Chapter 7 we considered the Data Protection Act requirements. In the Agreement it is important for the film company to ensure that the designer recognises their obligations under the Data Protection Act if they are to store or process personal data they acquire. The film company might seek an indemnity from the designer for unauthorised disclosure of such personal data which causes the film company to be in breach of the Data Protection Act and suffer financial penalty or loss.

It is often said that in litigation there are no winners except the lawyers. Certainly the costs of going to court can be prohibitive and so, even where there is a dispute that cannot be resolved by discussion between the film company and the designer, actual court proceedings should be avoided where possible. One way is to include an Alternative Dispute Resolution procedure in the Agreement. This is where both parties agree to appoint a mediator in the event of dispute in an attempt to reach agreement. It is a way to seek resolution without the costs of going to court. If the mediation cannot be concluded or if one party refuses to proceed on that route, then the other party can still sue in the courts for redress.

CHECKLIST

- Always ensure a comprehensive Website Design and Development Agreement is signed with the website designer.

- Carefully consider who owns what in terms of the intellectual property rights in the website.

- Check how payment for the website is to be made and that there are no hidden extras such as content management charges for the designer updating the website.

- Make sure the circumstances for termination of the Agreement are clear and what the consequences are for such termination.

- Include an Alternative Dispute Resolution clause.

FILM AND TELEVISION WEBSITE HOSTING AGREEMENT

It is becoming clear that, with the huge increase in internet usage in this country and around the world fuelled by high levels of broadband penetration, stress on the servers operated by the Internet Service Providers is acute. Now that most of the broadcast channels, including ITV, BBC and Channel 4, are placing large elements of their broadcast content online the internet networks are being hit significantly, threatening continuity of service. This trend of offering broadcast and film content online is only going to increase as compression technologies improve. The change will also be hastened by the availability of laptop computers which can now be characterised as media centres and not merely computing devices. As the PC market undergoes churn in terms of people replacing their PCs and laptops every two to three years, the ability to watch film and television programmes on laptops with high quality screens is greater. Peer-to-peer internet traffic now consumes around 70 per cent of bandwidth and promises to increase, with the entertainment industry embracing peer-to-peer for content distribution and the increasing popularity of personal audio and video players. Many in the internet industry predict that, as online film content becomes ubiquitous, so it is inevitable that a two-tier internet evolves. This would mean that, in order to reduce pressure on the networks, users might pay a standard rate for mainstream internet access but a premium rate if they want to access media-rich websites such as, for example, YouTube.

We have just looked at the key features in the relationship between the film company and its website designer. The next vital marriage is that of the film company and the Internet Service Provider which hosts its website. We will refer to that provider in this section as the hosting company. Website hosting services comprise the storage of a website and its content on a service provider owned or leased server.

It is the case that film and television content owners hold the power and to that extent there is huge opportunity for the industries in the new media age. The future will be aggregation for platform owners such as Internet Service Providers and mobile phone companies. From their perspective they want to secure one deal with a film company with, for example, 300 film titles rather than just one title. They want a product which will drive consumers to their service. There is much to play for. It is believed that in this country there are around 14.5 million households which currently have not adopted cable or digital television. This is the target market for the various platform owners. Similiarly, the film company will have essential demands to make on the platform owner.

Clearly the website operated by the film company must be capable of being supported continuously. It is likely that a range of services will be offered through it, each of which demand uninterrupted availability and access by the film audience. It is therefore of critical importance that the company has in place an Agreement with the provider of the hosting services which sets out clearly the service levels to be expected of that hosting company.

To assist with focusing on the primary issues the film company is likely to face, the following is a brief review of the issues to be covered in a Website Hosting Agreement.

Despite the need for continuity the film company will be asked by the hosting company to acknowledge that from time to time its systems, servers and equipment will be inoperative or partly operational due to mechanical breakdown, maintenance, hardware or software upgrades or other causes beyond its control. In each case proper notification by the hosting company must be given to the film company. Occasional problems of this kind might be tolerated by the film company. However, the seamless delivery of media content by the film company from its website is vital to its reputation and therefore repeated instances would be cause for termination of the relationship, as discussed below.

The hosting company will probably include a clause stating that it will not warrant that the hosting services are fit for the particular purposes the film company may require. This clause should be resisted by the film company if presented as part of the negotiations.

The hosting company will usually attempt to limit and restrict its legal and financial exposure to its client and may seek to limit its total financial liability to the value of the hosting services provided in relation to the performance of its obligations under the contract. Moreover, it may exclude liability for consequential loss which the film company might suffer as a result of interruption to the hosting services. An example might be if the film company has a commercial relationship with a third party company surrounding the film company's website. If the website is not operational due to the hosting company's error, the financial consequences to the film business may not simply be its own losses but also those of the third party company, who would look in the first instance to the film company for recovery of its losses. The film company must therefore look carefully at the contract to see if it contains exclusions of this kind.

The hosting company will exclude liability for the content provided by the film company.

The Agreement will make clear that it does not constitute any transfer of intellectual property rights which the film company has in the content it requires hosting.

The hosting company might want to use the film company logo or perhaps, if the film title or back catalogue consists of iconic or well-known titles or images, those depictions as well. The hosting company might want to include reference to the same in the marketing of its own services. If this is the case then the Agreement should state it clearly.

The hosting company should be asked to warrant that its services will be provided by appropriately qualified and experienced personnel using all reasonable skill and care.

The film company will usually be under a contractual obligation to confirm that it will install and maintain industry standard computer virus protection software and will take reasonable steps to ensure that any software it uses in conjunction with the hosting services will not damage or corrupt any system of the hosting company.

The film company will be requested to be solely responsible for dealing with any complaints about its content and online film audiences will not be directed to the hosting company in the event of any such complaints.

One very important aspect of the relationship – though surprisingly sometimes overlooked perhaps amid the enthusiasm at the start of the relationship – is how the parties can get out of the relationship. Each party's right to terminate the contract must be set out. The film company will be required to meet the hosting charges and all other obligations imposed by the contract. If it fails to do so the hosting company will seek to terminate the contract. Likewise the film company should insist on very tight service level obligations on the hosting company and if these are breached by it then a right to terminate on the part of the film company should be included. Usually the failure of service level obligations is addressed by way of service credits for failure. These may be expressed in financial terms in the form of stipulated amounts which trigger to varying degrees based on the time during which service is interrupted. This issue will in most cases be negotiated according to commercial strength. In other words a major television broadcaster will insist on very high levels of continuity on the part of the hosting service. For example, interactive programmes are very popular now. They often call for viewer participation by way of votes, which are a central element of the programme format. The television company may be offering a simultaneous online broadcast or other related interactive facility via its website while the programme is broadcast to the television audience in the usual way. Any failure of the service could render the programme success problematic, which itself may prejudice valuable programme sponsorship or advertising support. The level of continuity therefore demanded by the television company will be flawless and it would impose punitive penalties on the hosting company if the service were to fail. The ability for smaller film companies to leverage such penalties form the hosting company is likely to be far less.

As is usual in any commercial agreement between businesses, if either party goes into liquidation or threatens to be wound up, such an event will permit termination of the contract by the other party.

There will be an obligation on both the film or television company and the hosting company to maintain the confidentiality of the other's business information that has been revealed during the negotiation of the relationship and during the hosting arrangement.

As with all key commercial relationships between a film company and its strategic partners, full specialist legal advice should be obtained first. Remember that, whoever the music business deals with, they are themselves commercial entities and will seek to exclude or limit their own liability in the relationship as much as possible. In many cases it will be a question of bargaining power as to the extent such restrictions may govern.

MOBILE COMMUNICATIONS SERVICE PROVIDER AGREEMENT

Evidence suggests that consumers like television and they like mobile phones. Therefore convergence is inevitable. We are now in a world of blended media. The major broadcasters in the UK – BBC 1, ITV1 and Channel 4's E4 brand – are now available on mobile phones running at the same schedule as the conventional channels.

As the internet and mobile apparatus develop, an increasing range of content is being offered online by the film industry. Filmmakers see video-enabled iPods as pocket-sized alternative outlets for showcasing short films. Other models may use a combination of website downloads and SMS short codes with shared telephone short code numbers allocated to the film company by the provider of the service.

We will now consider a fairly sophisticated service operated by a film company whereby revenue is generated by the use of content delivery via, for example, mobile phones. This might be behind-the-scenes information about a film production, exclusive interviews with the cast, or other forms of unique content for which audiences might be willing to pay. If a film company is considering providing such content it will usually need to find a partner company to provide the premium rate numbers, SMS short codes, managed content or interactive voice recognition services to enable the film company to offer the content to its telephone callers. The relationship will require an Agreement setting out the obligations and responsibilities of each party. We will now examine some of the provisions one might expect to find in such an Agreement.

For ease of explanation we will call the provider of the service the 'Provider'. It is important to appreciate that such arrangements are complex and typically the Provider will not be the operator of the telecommunications system itself. The Provider will have to contract with such a company for the provision or management of interconnection and that contract falls beyond the scope of this book.

The Provider will almost certainly confirm that the services are not specifically designed for the film company and that the Provider is dependent on the telecommunications company and perhaps other third parties for the provision of the services. It will not therefore offer any assurances or guarantees.

The contract will usually continue until terminated by either party on notice in the case of termination for commercial reasons, or immediately if one party is in serious breach of its obligations. For example, the Provider will terminate the contract if it receives a complaint or objection from the telecommunications company, regulator, government or other official body about the film company's services. The same termination right applies if the Provider believes that the film company is allowiing, or is poised to allow, the services to be used for any unlawful purpose. The Agreement may also be terminated if the film company does not adhere to any code of conduct published by the mobile network operators such as O2, T-Mobile, Orange, Virgin, Vodafone or 3. The Agreement would also terminate immediately if either party goes into liquidation or threatens to do so.

Another cause for termination on the part of the Provider is inadequate financial performance of the service operated by the film company using, for example, the premium rate numbers. Usually a minimum monthly figure must be achieved by the film company, for example £100 per month.

The Provider may terminate the Agreement in the event of breach by the film company or it may restrict the service available to the business.

The film company will not have any ownership in the premium rate numbers or SMS short codes. In fact the SMS short codes will be used by other customers of the Provider.

The Provider may re-allocate numbers or codes where there are perhaps fewer than 20 calls per month to the premium rate numbers or SMS short codes for three or more consecutive months, or for other reasons for termination as described above.

The Provider will seek to limit its liability in a variety of ways. It will state that it cannot guarantee a fault-free service nor guarantee the capacity. It will not warrant that the equipment will be error free or that the network will be continuous or fit for the purposes of the film company.

The Provider will periodically need to suspend the service for the purpose of system maintenance and will, of course, give the film company reasonable notice of such suspension.

It will suspend, restrict or bar the services if at any time the number of calls to the premium rate numbers causes congestion or other disruption to the Provider's system. It can be seen that very clear dialogue must take place between the film company thinking of offering services to audiences via premium rate or SMS short codes and the Provider. These discussions will include likely levels of traffic. It would be little use to the film company if its mobile phone campaign was so successful that it caused disruption to the Providers' system and was suspended, causing annoyance to the film content consumer. Full discussion might reveal that the Provider might impose traffic restrictions on particular premium rate numbers to preserve service quality. The film company will be required under the Agreement to notify the Provider of any television- or radio-based advertising campaigns or other promotions that are likely to result in sudden peaks in calls or SMS traffic so as not to risk failure of the system.

It may be that the service offered by the film company requires specific licensing or approval. The Provider will require that the film company obtains all necessary approvals, licences and permissions from any Regulator or other body and that such permissions remain in force.

The Provider will want the right to monitor all services and record any calls made to the premium rate numbers or text sent to or from the SMS short codes used by the film company.

The film company will be required to supply to the Provider information and material from time to time requested, including advertising copy, promotional material and recorded messages, which the Provider may use for billing and credit checking purposes.

All advertising by the film company of the services it offers via the premium rate and SMS short code service must be approved in advance in writing by the Provider.

The film company will have to confirm that its content does not infringe any intellectual property rights belonging to a third party and that the content is not defamatory, libellous or illegal.

The Agreement will state that all advertising and promotional material used by the film company must comply with the relevant regulatory provisions relating to both the media within which the advert is placed and the content of the advert.

The film company will be required to have in place sufficient indemnity insurance in respect of the items it wishes to provide using the Provider's services.

The Provider will calculate its charges by reference to the data recorded or logged by it and not by the data recorded or logged by the film company. The Provider may provide the film company with a report or online statistics to give an indication of the traffic generated by the film company's campaign.

The Provider will include provisions relating to clawback of monies overpaid to the film company. In fact the Provider will usually have the ability to include a retention which is an amount to cover any actual or potential clawback.

The film company will be called upon to pay any fines levied by any regulatory body either on the Provider or the film company itself. The Provider will impose an administration charge for having to deal with such issues. The Agreement will also require the film company to hold harmless and indemnify the Provider against all liability which the film company incurs as a result of its service.

It may be seen that Agreements of this kind cover a variety of issues and they are likely to favour the Provider of the premium rate or SMS short code services. Clearly, the larger the film company and the greater the scale of the campaign it is embarking on, the more it is likely to be necessary to ensure equal balance of responsibilities and liability in the Agreement. If a film company is considering a launch of mobile services to its artists' fans to accompany its online activity, full legal advice must be obtained during the negotiation of the Agreement.

CHECKLIST

- Ensure that the relationship between the film company and its website designer is properly set out in a Website Development Agreement and includes precise terms covering intellectual property rights and any ongoing consultancy.

- Continuity of internet service is vital to the film company so ensure that a detailed Hosting Agreement is entered into which sets out service level guarantees on the part of the hosting company.

- If offering mobile services content, ensure that a comprehensive Agreement is in place between the provider of the premium rate or SMS short code services and the film company

CHAPTER 11

Strategic Agreements Between the Online Film Company and Content Aggregators

BACKGROUND

As the film industry embraces new media, film companies are seeking to leverage new platforms and audiences and are investing heavily in interactive development. The problem at this stage of development is how long it will take for consumers' habits to change.

Market sizing and projections in terms of examining the trends, threats and opportunities of new digital platforms facing content owners and producers as they move from traditional film distribution to new forms of digital distribution present very complex issues.

Some televisual genres could be tailor-made to cross over to new media platforms. Game shows, talent shows and reality shows are all naturally interactive and ideal for cutting down into bite-sized chunks for websites or mobile phones. Interactive television engages the viewer in a dialogue and takes them beyond the passive experience of watching television. It allows them to take part and make choices. However, other genres are more difficult. The audience of a game show or a reality show expects to interact with the programme: the audience of a scripted drama or sitcom does not.

Everyone associated with new media recognises that change is inevitable, but quantifying that change is difficult. This means that placing a value on digital rights is also uncertain. Filmmakers are attempting to assess what their digital rights are worth. Content platforms such as Internet Service Providers or mobile phone service providers adopt a stance of 'We don't know but come along with us and the future might be interesting'. They are therefore tending to offer the content owner revenue share deals where the values can be ring-fenced more easily. Undoubtedly, larger independent productions companies will have more influence to exploit their intellectual property rights with major Internet Service Providers, but many believe that the real test will simply be the quality of the content that determines the deals that can be secured.

It is certain that broadband connections in this country have outstripped pay TV subscriber adoption. The technology is evolving rapidly and in many instances the film company will not have the ability to develop new channels to market and offer the complete service to its target audience. Therefore it must enter into partner relationships with other companies that can support innovative formats and implement leading edge technology.

Who, then, is delivering film content online? The answer is a plethora of businesses. These include network operators or Internet Service Providers, telecommunication companies, mobile phone companies, technology companies such as Apple, television broadcasters such as the BBC, ITV and Channel 4, and brand extenders such as Tescos. It is a fragmented market. However, the issue is one of consumer adoption not technical ability.

Internet Service Providers recognise the potential for new media. They want to offer films, documentaries, music, comedy, drama and children's programmes – all at the touch of a button with the ability to pause, rewind and store content.

There is little doubt that digital distribution of films is going to become widespread as internet-based video-on-demand opportunities grow on the back of increasing broadband penetration and Hollywood studios put their weight behind consumer-focused online distribution as their DVD revenues begin to plateau. Online distribution enables a mix of viewing options including pay-per-view, video-on-demand and subscription-based video-on-demand as well as free, advertisement-driven films (see Chapter 12). The film company thus needs to explore new commercial opportunities.

In this chapter we will consider some strategic commercial relationships that the film company might enter into in order to maximise revenue from its digital presence.

LINKING AND REVENUE SHARE AGREEMENT (THE CLICK THROUGH REVENUE DEAL)

Needless to say, the internet is all about links. It is an established feature of websites to contain hyperlinks to other related websites and with broadband efficiency the visitor can move seamlessly from one site to another, gathering a wealth of information. For websites offering a commercial service there is much to be gained by the monetising of those relationships to other websites. As the convergence of technology and media advances with increased crossover of service and format the film company might well explore strategic relations with other parties providing different but complementary services. This will almost certainly involve a strategic relationship on a click-through revenue share basis.

In the film industry there is increased crossover of both platforms and service delivery. A film company can offer material promoting its titles which would include DVDs, trailer downloads and certain associated title merchandise. However, with branding of content being such a vital part of the publicity and advertising, the film company might need to source development of related digital products from other software disciplines. If those related products are offered online by their manufacturer or developer, there will be commercial merit in the film company entering into a strategic relationship to secure revenue from sales of the product which are attributable to a link from the film company website to the developer website.

The film company wishing to establish formal links with another commercial entity must embody the commercial basis of that relationship in a Linking and Revenue Share Agreement. In addition, a number of legal considerations should also form the content of that Agreement.

In this section we will take as an example such an online relationship between a film company website and a video games website. There has been a significant rise of MMOGs (massive multiplayer online games) and metaverses such as Second Life, so it is a useful example.

We have assumed that the film company will take a commission percentage on all sales of the video games achieved via the link from the film company website.

Typically the film company ('F'), with the assistance of the video games company ('V'), will agree to set up a connection with F's software to V's website. This link will provide a seamless connection and enable F's online audience to connect to, perhaps, the 'order' section or shopping basket of V's website. The Agreement will confirm that both F and V will be entitled to refer to each other as 'Alliance Partners' or some similar description to highlight their commercial connection in all their advertising and marketing material.

In our example we have envisaged that F will receive commission on sales of V's games. The Agreement will therefore deal with this arrangement and specify the commission rate. It will state that V will have the sole right and responsibility for processing all orders made by F's online consumer base. F will acknowledge that all contracts for the sale of the games to that audience are between V and the consumers and not F and the consumers.

It might be that V is free to set the price of the games, although in such a key relationship there could possibly be some agreement between F and V over pricing. Either way the actual pricing model needs to be set down in the Agreement.

V will be under an obligation to identify customers originating from F's website and log them as 'F&V customers' or an appropriate designation to reflect their nature. V will also be required to supply a monthly statement of all such transactions. The statement would need to show clearly all sales, refunds or deferred sales during that month. The statement would set out full details of the revenue achieved, the gross profit generated and, of course, the commission payable to F.

V would probably commit to paying F following receipt of an invoice from F, which invoice might be rendered on the first day of the calendar month for the previous calendar month. There would be an express exclusion of liability for V to make a payment to F in cases where full payment has not been made by a 'F&V customer' or where a refund has been given by V in relation to the same. The usual payment terms might apply – for example, 30 days from receipt of F's invoice.

By its nature an Agreement of this kind would doubtless be for a limited period. The pace of development of new technology means that products are superseded quickly. The term of the Agreement therefore needs to be made clear. It might be for a fixed term of two years. The Agreement must be capable of being brought to an end sooner by either party in certain specified circumstances. An obvious termination trigger would be if either F or V was in material breach of an obligation under the Agreement or if F or V enters into liquidation, or threatened liquidation, or some other form of insolvency-related arrangement. In such circumstances termination needs to be immediate. The Agreement would state that all commission payments due up to the date of termination must be met by V.

The matter of intellectual property is very important to both the media and software development industries. With the increased convergence of the two, examined elsewhere in this book, it is important to set clear the ownership rights of the various intellectual property elements which combine to perfect the relationship between F and V. Both F and V will retain all right to, title and interest in their names, logos, trademarks, service marks, copyrights and proprietary technology. The Agreement will provide for the granting of a revocable, non-exclusive, wordwide licence to use, reproduce and transmit their respective names, trademarks and proprietary software on their respective websites solely for the purpose of creating the links between the websites.

On the matter of intellectual property rights, the Agreement will also state that neither F or V shall copy, distribute, modify, reverse engineer or create derivative works from the other's works. For example, V will not do this as regards the musical content provided by F and F will not seek to develop its own version of V's online games. Each will offer an indemnity to the other that they have not infringed the intellectual property of any third party in the creation of their respective works and, further, that they are not in violation of any applicable law or regulation. This issue is important. The internet's global reach can mean that it would not be lawful to make certain products available in certain countries. It might be that the content of certain film works would be offensive to a particular region or jurisdiction. The same might be true of the video game. There could be issues of libel in both the film and the game content. Other commercial considerations where an indemnity should govern include misleading advertisement laws (see Chapter 12) or unfair competition laws. Given that both parties are operating their strategic relationship using internet technology, there would be an indemnity for computer viruses and other destructive programs.

It is possible that, as F and V seek to promote their joint arrangement, they make statements about each other's product to other commercial or media organisations. The precise ambit of what they each might say in relation to the promotion of the product would be dealt with under the terms of a joint marketing agreement rather than this Linking Agreement. However, in this Agreement there would be an indemnity against all liability, losses, damage and professional fees brought by a third party arising out of a breach or a representation made either F or V about either the film or the games.

V might seek to restrict its total financial exposure to F for any breach F is responsible for, to the total amount of commission paid by V to F in the calendar year of the date of the legal claim.

There would be a need to maintain confidentiality in relation to any information imparted or made available to the other as a result of the commercial relationship. This would be amplified in the Linking Agreement. Confidential

Information would be defined to include all non-public information concerning the business, technology and structures of the disclosing party. The receiving party would agree to keep the same in confidence and not permit any employee, agent or other person working under its direction to disclose or disseminate the information. Reasonable steps must be taken by both F and V to secure confidential information where storage is achieved by electronic means, which will almost certainly be the case.

Neither F nor V will be able to assign (transfer) the benefit of the Linking Agreement to any third party without the prior consent of the other party.

Finally, the Agreement will be expressed to be governed by English law.

An agreement of this kind will contain many more specific commercial terms agreed as between a film company and video games company based on the actual deal struck. However, the above review sets out some principal provisions a film company should address if considering a strategic internet linking deal with another party.

THE FILM CONTENT LICENCE AGREEMENT

There are numerous issues for the film company to consider if venturing into internet distribution of its content. These include: whether platform-agnostic rights deals should be entered into; understanding what the traditional platforms are doing to protect their interests; how the film company might overcome broadcaster protectionism; whether to accept rights bundles which include digital rights; and what scope exists for achieving lucrative digital rights agreement on both sides.

The film company must understand what its rights are and how it can structure deals to maximise commercial opportunities.

Gaining awareness of where the commercial opportunities lie and assessing which business models work best for the film company's content is paramount to successful rights exploitation. The company must know how it can take ownership of rights, rather than perhaps accepting fees up front. Is the chance of less upfront money for more long-term equity worth taking?

It needs to appreciate what rights it can realistically retain in current and future deals. When it should sell, who to and for how much? Do its traditional rights diminish when its digital rights are not included in the package?

All these issues are dealt with in the Licence Agreement between the content owner and the licensee of its content.

THE FILM CONTENT SOFTWARE LICENCE AGREEMENT

We have considered the position which governs the sale of merchandise from a film company website. However, there is increased pressure on film companies and the industry as a whole to fight the threat of technology with technology. This means developing new products or devising new marketing initiatives which offer the audience more than the simple DVD or even film download. It is possible that some form of internet-based technology application could be offered to audiences via a download. This might be software which enables an enhanced experience for the film audience interested in a particular title. If that offer is a software application, then the only way it can safely be made available to the user is by licensing it. In other words, the film company would retain its proprietary rights over the software but would grant the consumer a limited right to access and use the software.

The risk with any internet-based system is that the moment a new service is launched online it can be adopted around the world. Therefore, if the film company as content provider cannot manage an international roll out within a period of weeks, someone else could steal the market opportunity that has been created. The question then arises of how the film company can achieve legal protection for its web-based system. The answer lies in what is known as a web wrap software licence. The web wrap software licence has been devised to satisfy the needs of technology and mass marketing over the internet. The licence is to be used where it is almost impossible to obtain the signature of the end user to a licence before software is delivered unless an electronic signature is used. The next best thing is constructive acceptance of the licence terms.

As we noted in our review of contract formation online, the terms and conditions of the web wrap licence must appear on screen either at the ordering stage and/or before the software can be downloaded to ensure its full content can be read and accepted by the proposed end user.

The following are examples of typical provisions a film company might wish to include in its licence of internet software. Clearly, the precise terms of such a licence will be heavily influenced by the nature of the actual product being licensed and what it is designed to offer. Nonetheless our review serves as a helpful guide.

At the opening of the Licence Agreement there will be a statement advising the user that before they click on the 'I Accept' button at the end of the document and download the software they must carefully read the terms and conditions of the Licence Agreement. Further, by clicking on the 'I Accept' button and downloading the software they are consenting to be bound by and are becoming the licensee to the licence. They should be told that if they do not agree to all of the terms of the Licence they should click the 'I Do Not Accept' button and not download the software.

The Agreement would then confirm that when the user clicks the 'I Accept' button the film company grants them a non-exclusive, non-transferable licence for the software product, including any electronic documentation (the 'software'). Typically the licence would allow the user to use the software on a single computer system and will prevent its being transferred electronically from one computer to another or used over a network. Many young internet users are adept at finding ways to copy software and they routinely visit friends' homes and thus use a variety of computers. The licence will state that the software is not free or shareware and that there is a licence fee.

On accepting the licence the consumer will be asked to undertake not to copy or disassemble, decompile or reverse engineer the software. Nor must they translate, lease, modify, redistribute or sub-licence the software or create derivative works.

The film company would want to be free to create new versions or upgrades of the software. It would state that, whilst it has no obligation to notify existing licensees of those upgrades, new versions and/or upgrades will be made available at the same internet website from which the licensee downloaded the software. The cost of the upgrade would, of course, also be stated.

It is important to impose a restriction requiring the end user to agree not to display the software on a public bulletin board, the worldwide web or internet chat room, or by any other unauthorised means. In addition, the end user must be prohibited from using the software for any immoral, illegal or harmful manner, which would include the creation of any computer virus, Trojan horse or other destructive computer program.

It is highly likely that the film company will have either developed the software in-house or otherwise engaged the services of an external software developer. In either case the company may well have reserved the intellectual property rights in the product. However, if the product were, as is common, licensed from another company, perhaps the software developer, then clearly the film company would not own the intellectual property rights itself. On the basis that the film company does have title to the intellectual property, then it would wish to retain those rights in the Licence Agreement it is granting to its online end user. It would reserve all copyright, trademarks and other intellectual property rights subsisting or used in connection with the software. These would include all images, animations, audio and other identifiable material relating to the software.

The Licence Agreement must deal with the question of termination both at the instigation of the film company and of its online consumer. The Licence Agreement would state that the end user may terminate the Licence at any time by destroying the software and any documentation and that no licence fee is refundable. The Agreement should state that the film company may terminate the Licence Agreement at any time if the end user is found to be in breach of any of the terms.

ONLINE LICENCE BETWEEN FILM CONTENT PROVIDER AND COMMERCIAL WEBSITE OFFERING UPLOADED FILM CONTENT

This book examines the legal considerations which affect those associated with the film industry when using the internet commercially. The form and extent of such use will vary, with most film companies producing content distributed in much the same way as they have done for decades. They will have websites, but these are restricted to the offer of merchandise, title release news and other facilities. However, there is an increasing number of companies established solely for film promotion and distribution via the internet. Then there are the legitimate online film provider websites who simply make film catalogues available via the medium against payment.

In these examplary legal terms for a licence, we are envisaging that a filmmaker wishes to make available their film content over the internet by using an independent website operator for the purpose. There is, of course, nothing to prevent the filmmaker putting out their content over the internet themselves via a website developed for them. However, there are issues and costs around producing such a website and it is possible that the filmmaker wishes to get their content promoted over the internet using a website operated and promoted via another organisation. For the purposes of our example, then, we will consider this use of an external website.

At the time of writing the European Union is considering the introduction of an online copyright licence. The creators of online film content would be able to secure a single pan-European copyright licence. The proposal by the European Commission is designed to boost the growth of legitimate online content services in the EU and close the gap with the United States in webcasting and streaming. The main aim is to ensure that more royalties are distributed to rights holders across national borders.

The Agreement we will examine next is intended to cover the arrangement by which an online company wishes to use a filmmaker's film content on its website and sell those films via the website. The scenario envisages an online film business offering to promote and make available to the public film works posted to it by filmmakers. As we have seen in Chapter 3, the website will require full legal terms and conditions which the film-buying website visitor will need to click through before completing the purchase. The following review is of the terms of the licence that will govern the relationship between the company and the filmmaker for the provision of the film content to the web company.

The filmmaker thus agrees to licence certain film content to the web company for exploitation via the internet. The filmmaker will grant the web company the non-exclusive right for an agreed period of time to exploit the film content throughout a specified territory via the internet. This right will also permit the web company to make any alterations to the content technically required to make the film content available to the user via the medium. Typically combined with this right will be a right for the web company to use any promotional material from the film. Further, the web company will want to retain data relating to the filmmaker on a database and deal with such data for the purpose of marketing the film content. The web company will gain ownership of the database of contacts to whom the filmmaker's film is distributed that it builds up.

The web company will want the ability in its sole discretion to choose not to exploit the film or any promotional material if, in its reasonable opinion, it is necessary for legal, technical or marketing reasons. It might also attempt to include a provision which states that if the filmmaker is unable to make their film content available to the public due to the act or default of the web company for a specified period (for example, 30 days), then the only remedy open to the filmmaker would be termination of the online licence by notice in writing.

The issue of royalties is fundamental to film distribution. Typically the internet licence will make clear that all royalty payments due to the filmmaker will be processed in accordance with the terms contained in the licence. The web company will then deduct and retain the royalty from the gross revenues achieved by the sale of the film via the website.

There are other commercial terms which one would expect to see included in the online film licence between the web company and filmmaker just as they would appear in more traditional agreements. Thus, the web company would commit to the provision of accounts to the filmmaker within a specified period of time, perhaps twice a year. The accounts would cover the preceding period and be accompanied by the appropriate payment due to the filmmaker.

The web company will want to obtain certain warranties from the filmmaker in relation to the film content which they agree to make available. First, the web company would usually want the filmmaker to warrant that he or she is free to enter into the Agreement and has attained the age of 18. In addition, the web company would want a warranty that the filmmaker has not entered into any arrangement which might conflict with the licence to be granted and is under no restriction or prohibition which might prevent the filmmaker from performing any of their obligations under the licence. The web company can do its best to mitigate its exposure by the imposition of such a warranty.

The web company should add a provision requiring that the production values rendered by the filmmaker shall be of first class technical and artistic standard.

Another warranty required would be that the services rendered by the filmmaker are original and shall not, under the laws in force in any part of the world, be obscene, blasphemous, defamatory of any person, or infringe any right of copyright or right of privacy or performers' rights or indeed any other right of a third party. It has been noted elsewhere in this book that it is not, however, possible to exclude liability for defamation. In addition, the filmmaker shall render the services to the best of his or her skill and ability in a professional and workmanlike manner in full cooperation with the web company and all people engaged by the web company.

The web company would also need to have absolute discretion on the issue of promotion and advertising of the film and all other related matters.

Another desirable clause the web company should include in its licence agreement is an indemnity by the filmmaker. This would be an agreement to indemnify the web company fully against all claims and any associated costs arising as a result of any breach by the filmmaker or non-performance of any of the filmmaker's warranties and obligations under the licence agreement.

The web company would impose an obligation of confidentiality on the filmmaker in terms of confidential information gathered by virtue of entering into the licence agreement.

The details of exactly which film works are to be licensed to the web company for online distribution would usually be set out in a schedule to the licence agreement.

The licence agreement outlined above can be offered on the film website itself with the filmmaker agreeing to its terms by clicking through the terms, as discussed elsewhere. In any event, under the provisions of the E-Commerce Regulations 2002 ,the full terms of the licence must be capable of being printed off in hard copy.

THE ONLINE FILM MAGAZINE SUBSCRIPTION AGREEMENT

Film companies are considering ways in which to use their websites to offer an array of exclusive content. This is both to attract more users to the website on a regular basis and retain their loyalty and also because the very nature of the medium permits the provision of dynamic content which cannot be made available in any other way. Much of this material is offered free and other merchandise or advance title release information may be offered for sale, albeit at special rates. Another source of revenue for the website is the production of an online magazine or journal which contains the latest news or in-depth interviews with the title's cast or production team, together with other content of direct interest to the filmgoer. This might be offered free but can also be delivered via the website on a paid-for model. Online journals offer a means of monetising the website audience by providing further advertising and sponsorship opportunities.

For example, in 2005 the artist Robbie Williams launched an online subscription service transforming him into a retailer and cashing in on intellectual property ranging from images to live footage and interviews. The website is thus a full commercial business rather than a marketing strategy.

Subscribers have access to a library of over 1,000 images and exclusive behind the scenes video clips, together with every Robbie Williams video.

In this section we will review some of the items which a provider of an online film journal might include in the legal terms which would be posted on the website. A common example of the use of this online bulletin is by a film company to its online audience. However, online journals might be offered by other commercial providers connected with the film industry. The same considerations will apply whoever makes the magazine available and the guidance provided in this section should thus be read accordingly. Once again it is important to remember that in so doing the provider is asking the website visitor to enter into a legally binding contract and, as we have seen, a contract must contain a number of conditions for it to both fulfil the legal criteria in English law and also safeguard the interests of the content provider. In common with the strategic legal agreements previously discussed in this book, there are significant consumer law protections which must be adhered to by the provider, since it is envisaged that the online magazine will be targeted at a consumer audience, and more than likely a young one. These laws govern any contract with consumers and not merely those conducted online.

The following review was prepared on the assumption that the magazine will be subscribed to on a single-user licence, that is, offered to, say, individual fans to be accessed by them against their personal password. Multi-user or corporate-wide licences can be prepared but these require additional provisions not dealt with in this work. The subscriber would need to be pushed through the legal terms and conditions when they first register their details to subscribe to the journal in the manner of a 'click wrap' contract. Thus the website must be designed in such a way as to make sure that the legal terms must be clicked through before the subscription application can be completed. Likewise, the requirements of the E-Commerce Regulations 2002 apply (see Chapter 4).

First, it is vital to ensure that the subscriber has legal capacity to enter into the contract and they must therefore be over the age of 18 to subscribe or obtain parental authority to sign up for the magazine.

The film company will be offering a non-exclusive, non-transferable licence to use the subscription service. Usually that licence will permit the electronic display of the material on a single computer by the visitor, or the downloading or printing of one copy of the journal.

It is important to build in some protection in terms of restricting the use of the material. So, for example, clear statements confirming that the user cannot store, download, transmit, copy or reproduce the content must be incorporated. The user must not be allowed to sub-licence, lease or assign the rights in the content to any other person. They should be prevented from making the journal content available on a network or allowing anyone else to use the content other than in accordance with the licence terms and conditions now being put before them.

The need to specify that the online journal is for their private non-commercial use is clear. If the film company establishes that any of the above limitations on use have been breached by the user, then the company must have the ability to terminate or suspend access to the magazine.

As the subscriber is being asked to pay for the journal, full information on how payment is to be made must be included. The price needs to be fixed for the date and time of the order and needless to say it is incumbent upon the film company to ensure that prices are maintained accurately and, if the subscription price increases, the latest detail is posted to the website.

As considered elsewhere, remember that the film website is not an offer for sale of any content or products available by accessing it. Thus the proper approach is to make clear in the subscription terms that the film company is entitled to refuse any subscription request placed by the online subscriber. An electronic confirmation must be sent to the user only when the subscription request is actually accepted by the film company. Now, suppose the user signs up to receive the magazine. Is it possible for them to cancel their order under the provisions of the Distance Selling Regulations 2000 (see Chapter 8)? The answer is no. An online magazine contract is not subject to the seven-day cancellation right. It is certainly open to the film company to elect to offer a cancellation option within a prescribed time scale, but that would be simply a matter of commercial gesture rather than a legal obligation.

Next we come to the matter of collecting the personal information about the subscriber. This is likely to consist of their full name, postal address, e-mail address, telephone number and almost certainly their age and gender. Such data is, of course, a valuable resource to the film company. However, the precise use to which the personal details might be put by the company must be made clear. As the internet enables highly targeted and real-time information to be delivered a film company might, for example, wish to offer different versions of the content to their subscribers according to age and gender. The personal information thus given will allow sophisticated marketing strategies of this kind and the online questionnaire will probably be far more detailed to obtain a precise user profile. It should be the responsibility of the subscriber to give accurate information.

The issue of personal profile also arises in geographical considerations. Major film companies are global concerns, but even more modest companies might have correspondent relations with other companies in other countries. It might be that the film company wishes to offer specific content to users in particular countries based, perhaps, on an understanding of the buying behaviour previously displayed by those users, or for very cogent legal reasons. In any event, the question of whether to accept subscribers only from the United Kingdom or from other countries via the website needs to be addressed. The better view is to restrict access to UK subscribers only: if it is intended to offer variations of the content to non-UK residents then those visitors should be directed to alternative arrangements. The geo-filtering technology discussed in Chapter 5 is one method by which this can be achieved. However, the geographical restriction should also be made clear in the legal terms.

The film company must therefore state that they have used their best endeavours to ensure that the content complies with English law but make no representations that the service is appropriate to locations outside the UK. A statement to the effect that if the magazine or any products made available in it infringe any applicable law in another country then the user is not authorised to view the magazine and must exit immediately.

A clause stating that English law will govern the contract is essential.

The journal may well feature further web links to other websites referred to in the text of a particular story about a title or perhaps the actors. It is important to include an exclusion clause stating that the film company makes no representations about any other websites which the subscriber might access through the journal, that those other websites are not necessarily endorsed by the film company and that no liability for financial loss or any other damage will be accepted by the company if the user suffers the same by virtue of acting on information or viewing the content of those other sites. As we have seen elsewhere, however, although this exclusion will work in the context of certain possible areas of harm, such as someone suffering poor service or non-supply of merchandise from that other website, it will not shut out any liability on the film company for defamatory or offensive material displayed on that other website. Thus, the obligation on the film company to constantly monitor the content of websites linked to their site is significant.

As with any internet service there are many things that can disrupt access to the network and over which the film company has little control. Therefore, the website must make clear that the subscription service cannot be guaranteed continuously or without interruption and liability cannot be accepted for periods of downtime. Obviously there are questions of reasonableness here. The user is paying for a service delivered over the internet and they have reasonable expectation that they will be able to access it at times of their choosing. If the service were to suffer repeated interference, then a user would be well within their rights to demand cancellation and return of their subscription fee. No exclusion clause will protect a film company in such cases.

Certainly one would wish to include exclusions for financial loss that might be suffered by a subscriber indirect or consequential loss or damage, or loss of data, profit, or business alleged to have been suffered by the user. The film company would also want to make clear that it will not be responsible for computer viruses or infections which the user claims were contracted via the website. The subscriber must be made aware that it is their own responsibility to ensure that their computer system meets necessary technical specifications both to use the service and to view it with the benefit of anti-virus and other security check software.

CHAPTER 12

Online Advertising and Promotion of Film and Television Titles and Merchandise

BACKGROUND

Advertisement-funded content is the becoming the mainstay of online media distribution. Film and television internet distribution is no exception. Added to this is the huge increase in advertising spend on the internet. In 2006 major advertisers set aside much more of their budget for digital advertising. Television advertising is suffering at least in part because of this trend. It is a development whose effects are unlikely to diminish in the years ahead. It is founded on the levels of internet use in this country and the penetration of broadband in the homes of consumers. There is also a generation change upon us. Many young people returning from school or college no longer switch on the television. Instead they log on to the internet on their PC.

As broadband continues to penetrate the consumers' homes, online film and television distribution will become more popular. One option that will become part of the range of viewing experiences will be free, advertisement-driven films.

We have seen that it is vital for the film company to understand the precise nature of its online service. Once established, the legal terms of use can be properly drafted. The same precision in terms of online service is needed when it comes to the matter of promotion of the film title. The internet has radically changed the nature of marketing and advertising, just as it has changed the media industry in general. There are opportunities for promotion using viral marketing techniques which no one could have foreseen even two or three years ago. The use of social networking websites such as YouTube has created vast markets for film content and in the main user-generated content. These websites have proved remarkably effective in spreading a message simply by their users posting and transmitting messages about the film or sending the film content itself. In effect, the audience does the marketing for you. The implications in terms of reduced costs are easy to grasp. However, for every viral marketing success other channels remain necessary for the film company to deploy to promote its content.

There are models emerging based on the understanding that a piece of video can go anywhere on the internet and that it can be accompanied by a piece of advertising to that video and the revenue shared with the creator. The content creator splits the advertisement revenue perhaps 50/50 after the syndicater, who is the person presenting the content, has taken perhaps 20 per cent off the top. Once the advertisement has been attached to the video, the creator can distribute its content anywhere on the internet, including peer-to-peer networks.

As an aside, a number of digital agencies, in addition to offering website development services, also provide related internet services such as viral marketing campaigns, search engine optimisation, and pay per click advertising services. Advice should be taken on the effect of the service level agreements which such agencies seek to impose.

In this chapter we will consider the controls that exist in the UK on the use of advertising via the internet and mobile telephones.

A film company's advertising on the internet will be interactive and based on a model in which the customer comes to the company. Until the advent of the internet, interactive advertising or marketing activity had been conducted face-to-face. The worldwide web enables film companies to engage their consumers in the advertising itself.

A major challenge to film advertisers over the next decade will be finding ways to fully utilise this capability. Involving the online consumer in the advertising message can build long-term customer commitment.

Still the most common form of internet advertising is 'banner advertising'. Banner advertisements are no longer just static files. They may include animation, direct response and other interactivity. Web advertising is fairly simple in concept. The company decides it wants to place a banner advertisement on a website: it negotiates with the owner of the website. Usually, advertising rates are based on a certain cost per thousand impressions (CPM).

These impressions are measured by the owner of the website based on the number of times the banner is seen by visitors. At the end of the period, the website owner invoices the advertiser. It is calculated by multiplying the CPM by the number of impressions during that period.

Before considering online advertising, it is well to briefly set out the legal background to advertising production in the UK. In this country, advertising is regulated by voluntary codes. There are also many statutes which affect advertising.

THE BRITISH CODE OF ADVERTISING, SALES PROMOTION AND DIRECT MARKETING

The British Code of Advertising, Sales Promotion and Direct Marketing is now in its eleventh edition and came into force on 4 March 2003. It replaces all previous editions. It is the principal voluntary code in the UK and is drawn by the Committee of Advertising Practice.

The Advertising Standard Authority (ASA) is charged with the duty of monitoring compliance with the Code. The ASA is independent.

The Code applies to traditional media such as advertisements in newspapers, magazines and mailings but it also covers e-mails, text transmissions and other electronic material. In addition, the Code governs advertisements in non-broadcast electronic media including online advertisements in paid-for space, for example, banner and pop-up advertisements.

Therefore, a film company wishing to embark on an advertising campaign using e-mail, text messaging or the internet must abide by the provisions of the Code.

We will now examine the principal terms of the Code as they apply to an online film company. It is important to appreciate that the ambit of the Code is wide and it does not simply apply to advertisements in the traditional sense. The Code contains various definitions. For example, products which fall within its domain encompass goods, services, ideas, opportunities, prizes or gifts. Promotions are also covered. Thus, a film company wishing to offer a prize to win title merchandise via its website or running an online opportunity to claim a DVD gift, must comply.

There are some general rules which apply to an online, e-mail or text promotion or advertisement for film merchandise or services. These include:

- all marketing communications should be legal, decent, honest and truthful;

- all marketing communications should be prepared with a sense of responsibility to consumers and to society;

- all marketing communications should respect the principles of fair competition generally accepted in business.

TESTIMONIALS

There are many other requirements, for example, on the matter of testimonials and endorsements. A film company should hold signed and dated proof, including a contact address, for any testimonial it uses. Unless they are genuine opinions taken from a published source, testimonials should be used only with the written permission of those giving them. The testimonial must relate to the film product being advertised. Testimonials alone do not constitute substantiation and the opinions expressed in them must be supported, where necessary, with independent evidence of their accuracy. Fictitious testimonials should not be presented as though they are genuine.

There are clear guidelines on the protection of privacy of people the film company might wish to associate with the online or mobile advertisements. If referring to people with a public profile – for example, a well-known actor – references that accurately reflect the contents of books, articles or films may be acceptable without permission. Prior permission may not be needed when the marketing communication contains nothing that is inconsistent with the position or views of the person featured. However, if implying any personal approval of the advertised product, the online film company should recognise that those who do not wish to be associated with the product may have a legal claim.

PRICING

On the matter of pricing, any internet, mobile content or text advertising must ensure that stated prices should be clear and should relate to the product advertised. The film company must ensure that prices match the products illustrated in, for example, the photograph in the advertisement.

All prices quoted in marketing communications addressed to the public should include VAT and other non-optional taxes and duties imposed on all buyers.

A recommended retail price (RRP) or similar used as a basis of comparison should be genuine: it should not differ significantly from the price at which the product is generally sold. Film DVDs offered via the website of the film company at a discount from the RRP in shops, for example, must show a genuine reduction.

AVAILABILITY OF MERCHANDISE OR SERVICES

The film company must make it clear if stocks are limited. Products must not be advertised unless marketers can demonstrate that they have reasonable grounds for believing that they can satisfy demand. If the merchandise becomes unavailable, the film company will be required to show evidence of stock monitoring, communications with outlets and swift withdrawal of marketing communications whenever possible.

Merchandise which cannot be supplied should not normally be advertised as a way of assessing potential demand unless it is clear that this is the purpose of the marketing communication.

The film company must not use the technique of switch selling, where its sales staff criticise the advertised merchandise or suggest that it is not available and recommend the purchase of a more expensive alternative. They should not place obstacles in the way of purchasing the merchandise or delivering it promptly.

GUARANTEES

If the online film company is offering a guarantee it will be legally binding on it. The word 'guarantee' should not be used in a way that could cause confusion about consumer's legal rights. Any substantial limitations on the guarantee should be spelled out in the marketing communication. Before commitment, the online consumer should be able to obtain the full terms of the guarantee from the film company. Once again this brings in to question the practice of sending mobile broadcast advertisements which might have limitations on screen size or size of content transmitted. In such cases clear reference to the film company's website and the legal terms and conditions which appear on the website must be made.

If there is a money back guarantee, the film company must provide a cash refund or cheque promptly to those claiming redress under the offer.

Remember that it is necessary for the film company to ensure that its target users recognise that the message is a marketing communication. The e-mail message or mobile broadcast should be designed and presented in such a way that it is clear that they are marketing communications. Unsolicited e-mail marketing communications should be clearly identifiable as marketing communications without the need to open them.

ONLINE SALES PROMOTIONS

As stated above, the Code also applies to sales promotions and regulates the nature and administration of promotional marketing techniques. Those techniques usually involve providing a range of direct or indirect additional benefits, usually on a temporary basis, designed to make merchandise or services more attractive to purchasers.

The film company must conduct any promotion online or by mobile equitably, promptly and efficiently and should be seen to deal fairly and honourably with consumers. They should avoid causing unnecessary disappointment.

The film company wishing to promote merchandise or services should be able to demonstrate that it has made a reasonable estimate of likely response and that it was capable of meeting that response. Using phrases such as 'subject to availability' does not relieve promoters of the obligation to take all reasonable steps to avoid disappointing online participants.

The film company should not encourage consumers to make a purchase or series of purchases as a precondition to applying for promotional items if the number of those items is limited.

If the company is unable to supply demand for a promotional offer because of an unexpectedly high response or some other anticipated factor outside its control, it should offer refunds or substitute products.

The online or mobile promotion should be conducted under proper supervision and adequate resources should be made available to administer them. The film company should allow adequate time for each phase of the promotion – distributing the goods, collecting wrappers and the like – and announcing results. It is important to bear in mind that online and mobile promotions are capable of immediate response by consumers and that is their appeal to both film company and online audience. However, that means the film company must be able to fulfil with similar speed.

A free offer may be conditional on the purchase of other items. The consumer's liability for costs should be made clear in all material featuring the offer. An offer should be described as free only if consumers pay no more than:

a) the minimum, unavoidable cost of responding to the promotion, for example, the current public rates of postage, the cost of telephoning up to and including the national rate or the minimum, the unavoidable cost of sending an e-mail or SMS text message;

b) the true cost of delivery.

The film company should not charge for packing, handling or administration.

ESSENTIAL CONDITIONS FOR AN ONLINE PROMOTION

An online promotion should specify the following detail clearly before any purchase (or before or at the time of entry or application), if no purchase is required:

• how to participate, including significant conditions and costs and any other major factors reasonably likely to influence consumers' decisions or understanding about the promotion;

• the start and closing dates if applicable for purchases and submissions of entries or claims. Prize promotions and promotions addressed to or targeted at children always need a closing date;

• any geographical restrictions which apply should be stated and any other restrictions such as personal (for instance, age, or technological restrictions), for example, whether the purchase is only available by e-mail response and not text message. The film company should state any need to obtain permission to enter from an adult or employer.

SENDING ELECTRONIC MARKETING MESSAGES TO UNDER 16S

Special care needs to be taken when film promotions are addressed to children (people under 16) or when products intended for adults fall into the hands of children. Given that many actors have a large following of fans under 16, it is particularly important that the film company understands its obligations when sending electronic promotional messages.

The way in which children perceive and react to marketing communications is influenced by their age, experience and the context in which the message is delivered. So marketing communications which are acceptable for young teenagers will not necessarily be acceptable for young children. The film company therefore needs to take that into account.

Marketing communications addressed to, targeted at or featuring children should not exploit their credulity, loyalty, vulnerability or lack of experience. Children should not be made to feel unpopular or inferior for not buying the advertised product. They should not be made to feel that they are lacking in loyalty if they do not buy or do not encourage others to buy a particular product.

The advertisement should make it easy for them to judge the size, characteristics and performance of any product advertised and to distinguish between real-life situations and fantasy.

Adult permission should be obtained before they are committed to purchasing complex and costly products.

Promotions addressed to or targeted at children should not encourage excessive purchases in order to participate and, among other things, should contain a prominent closing date.

PENALTIES FOR BREACHING THE CODE

There is a much stricter regime relative to advertising regulations in contrast to the general law. A film company's advertisement claims require a level of justification in excess of that necessary for its editorial matter.

There are penalties for breaching the Code. If an online advertisement breaches the Code, the ASA will ask a film company to withdraw or amend its advertisement. Other sanctions include adverse publicity, the refusal of further space, removal of trade incentives and finally legal proceedings.

These sanctions are effected by referrals from the ASA to the Office of Fair Trading (OFT) under the Control of Misleading Advertisements Regulations 1988 (CMAR). The OFT can obtain an injunction against a film company to prevent it from repeating the same or similar claims in future advertisements.

The first problem which internet advertising highlights is the proper application of Advertising Standards in the right circumstances. The distinction between advertising material and editorial on a website can become blurred. This is exacerbated by the seamless linking of pages on the web, which renders it difficult to separate the two. This difficulty may lead to the inadvertent extension of advertising content restrictions to editorial content.

At the time of writing, there is no reported case concerning how an English court would approach the question. The issue was considered in the Irish case of *Dunnes Stores Limited v. Mandate*:

> *The case was founded on the Irish equivalent to the UK Control of Misleading Advertising Regulations 1988. A trade union representing a claimant's work force placed and advertisement in the National Press seeking to justify strike action by the Union's members over Christmas pay. The Irish Supreme Court held that the trade union's advertisement had nothing to do with the promotion of the supply of goods or services and so was not 'advertising'.*

When considering advertising and the internet, the most vexing issue is jurisdiction. The difficulty in properly regulating electronic commerce advertising lies trying to apply national frameworks of laws and regulations to adverts disseminated to the world at large. An online advertisement is, in theory, subject to the laws of every country in which it is accessed by an internet user. Thus far the ASA have focused on websites which originate in the UK. If it is faced with a foreign website, it may be able to refer the complaint to an equivalent regulatory body in the foreign jurisdiction.

The breach of non-domestic regulations as a result of the global 'reach' of the internet was illustrated in *United States v. Thoms*, a US court case.

> *In that case, the operators of a pornographic electronic bulletin board in California were convicted of criminal obscenity laws by a federal court in Tennessee. The conviction was founded on Tennessee standards of decency.*

At present there is no international unanimity on the issue of which country's law applies to internet advertising. The approach that seems to be adopted is that the laws of the country of 'publication' will apply, that is, the country in which there is evidence of 'directed' activity. This is illustrated by an incident involving the English-registered Virgin Atlantic Airways:

> *In 1996 Virgin was fined by the US Department of Transportation for a misleading advertisement on its UK server. The inaccuracy related to the quoting of erroneous fares and listing a fare that was no longer available on flights from the USA.*

The simple inclusion of information on the film company's website will not of itself be conclusive evidence of directed activity if there is something about the information making it clear it is targeted at customers in a particular country.

The language of an advertisement may be relevant to an extent. A disclaimer contained on the website may help to clarify who is included in the target audience. An example might be 'this offer is only available for consumers in France'. Such a disclaimer will, however, be construed narrowly and have no legal effect in some countries.

Whilst it will be impractical to obtain legal clearance in every jurisdiction throughout the world, there are some general principles to adopt.

- Obtain legal and trademark clearance in each target country and in countries in which the film company has a presence or assets.

- On a purely practical level, the film company might consider how costly it might be to change its online advertisement if it should be challenged.

- Would a competitor in fact be able to prove actual damage?

Finally, it may well be that the authorities in a given country will take a 'laissez-faire' approach to an internet advertisement.

If the film company engages the services of an advertising agency, the issue of the film company's internet advertising strategy must be discussed fully with the agency. The risks that a film company could incur liability for breach of foreign advertising regulation makes it essential for the contract with the agency to lay down clear lines of responsibility for ensuring legal compliance of advertising materials.

THE INTERNET FILM ADVERTISING AGREEMENT

There has been a huge increase in the acquisition of internet companies by larger media groups, predicated on the strong growth in internet advertising. This compares to traditional media activities such as television advertising, which is recording revenue decreases. The business world is now recognising that internet advertising is no longer a fantasy but an integral part of media businesses.

A significant development of the commercialisation of the internet has been the commercial sponsorship of websites. Website marketing and advertising are extremely important to a successful e-commerce strategy – one only has to reflect on the plethora of television advertisements which promote corporate and retail websites.

Usually such promotion is part of a wider advertising campaign. A film company might wish to sell rights to advertise on its website to others. This advertising can be in the form of banner adverts, hyperlinks and browser windows which start automatically. It might wish to distinguish between a 'sponsor', who is entitled to a more prominent place on the website, and other advertisers, who will receive lesser billing.

From the point of view of the advertiser, it will want to be clear not only about the rights it receives in isolation but also its position within the hierarchy of rights.

If a film company is entering into an arrangement with another company to enable that other company to advertise on its website, the Internet Advertising Agreement should cover the following:

> **Rights.** The rights being granted in respect of the film website should be determined. Is the advertiser to have exclusive rights? Are there categories of advertising within which the advertiser will have exclusivity, for example, that it will be the only video games developer on the site?

> **Payment structure and triggers.** It should be considered whether payment will be calculated on a base fee, per display, click-through or upon ultimate sale.

> **The responsibilities of the advertiser** in relation to appropriateness of adverts should be clearly understood.

> **Licences.** It would be prudent to enter into a limited licence for the use of graphics and/or text and trademark used in the advertisements.

> **Inclusion of indemnities** to limit liability should be considered.

> **Termination of the Agreement** should be clear. In addition, the Agreement should set out what will happen on termination. Usually, materials should be destroyed and webpages changed. If the Agreement is terminated at short notice, all payments due under the same should become immediately due and payable.

> **Nature of relationship between the advertiser and the film company.** The Agreement will only be for advertising cooperation. It

should state clearly that it does not create an agency or joint venture between the parties.

Positioning and size. An advertiser will wish to specify where on the website its advertisement will appear. The form and size of the advert relative to other text and other graphics should be clear. Internet advertising involves the consideration of the working of hypertext mark-up language (HTML) and the operating web browsers which will be used to access the sites. An advertiser might wish to set up the technical details of how, in particular, its logo is created so as to ensure that it both downloads at an acceptable speed and is attractive.

Updating. Some advertisers may want some contractual assurance that the webpage itself will be changed over time to keep up with new versions or releases of relevant browsers or, conversely, that the webpage will remain useable with older browser versions.

Website promotion obligations. If a website relates to a campaign by a film company in other media, advertisers may wish to have assurances about the promotion of the website within that campaign, such as by the inclusion of the website URL (uniform resource locator) on posters and other forms of advertising. Conversely, and particularly where there is one major sponsor, the film company might wish to oblige that sponsor to promote the website as part of the sponsor's own advertising.

Hypertext links. Both the film company and the advertiser will have concerns relating to the hypertext links from the advertisement to the advertiser's own web page. Advertisers will want to make sure that the link is correctly created and the website owner is obliged to update it correctly if there is a change in the URL of the advertiser's website. The advertiser might also wish to ensure that the link can be triggered either from the text message or a graphic. The film company should ensure that the link to the advertiser's website will not give rise to any liability to third parties for defamation.

Intellectual property. Advertisers will wish to specify the extent of the right of the film company to use any trade or service marks on the site and to ensure that it applies the marks consistently with any standard guidelines. The form of the advertising in general may concern the advertiser and they will wish to have prior approval of relevant copy. The film company should seek an indemnity in respect of third party claims arising from use of the advertiser's marks on the internet.

Information about visitors to the site. It will be of interest to both the advertiser and the film company just who visits the website. This is because the film company will need to justify its advertising rate card. The advertiser will need to judge whether the film company's webpages are an appropriate place to advertise.

RULES RELATING TO RINGTONE SALES

It is worth making a brief review of recent rules which, although targeted at mobile phone operators, have relevance to a film company, given the increased convergence of technology. In Chapter 2 we considered the potential problems when contracting with children and teenagers. As a result of concern expressed about the manner in which mobile phone ringtones are made available, recent changes have been introduced by the mobile telephone operators. The safeguards were as a result of the Crazy Frog ringtone discussed earlier (Chapter 2, p. 13). The mobile operators recognise that there is a need for effective controls that help consumers from becoming victims of misleading advertising and which set out clearly what is expected of content providers. O2, 3, Orange, T-Mobile and Vodaphone have all introduced the safeguards at network level. The new rules include the following:

- A standard message which includes details of service charges and billing frequency must be prominently displayed within any form of advertising for a subscription text services. In the case of television advertising, this new standard message must be permanent and static for the full duration of the advert and be accompanied with a voiceover.

- A mobile phone user joining a subscription text service must be sent a free reply text message from the content provider confirming the user's subscription commitment. The service operator must also provide a standard or free rate customer helpline number and include this number in the reply text message.

- All mobile phone users joining a subscription text service must be sent a notification text message either monthly or when £20 has been spent on that service, whichever comes first. The text must remind the user how to unsubscribe.

- All service operators must operate a website which includes terms and conditions for the service.

These new safeguards are in addition to the existing consumer protection rules contained in the Independent Committee for the Supervision of Standards of Telephone Information Services (ICSTIS) Code of Practice. They also build on the common 'STOP' command introduced recently by the mobile phone industry to enable customers to cancel subscription services by texting the word 'STOP' to the text short code related to their service. The 'STOP' command will now be extended to cover any form of text-, WAP- or media messaging-based marketing to enable consumers to stop the receipt of any marketing messages.

ICSTIS has also introduced a prior-permission requirement for open-ended services that can cost users more than £20 in total. Permissions will only be granted if service providers demonstrate that their services and advertising material meet certain standards designed to prevent consumer confusion and harm.

THE PRODUCERS ALLIANCE FOR CINEMA AND TELEVISION (PACT) HEADS OF AGREEMENT

In 2006 a deal was agreed between C4, ITV and the BBC and the production companies' body, Producers' Alliance for Cinema and Television (PACT). It allows broadcasters to embrace the internet.

Channel 4's deal gives it a 30-day post-transmission window in which to exploit programmes across all platforms, with producers getting a share of revenue, or a 'royalty' payment if the services are offered to viewers free of charge.

ITV also struck a deal with PACT that will let it rerun programmes on all platforms for up to a month after broadcast. The BBC's deal, the first to be struck, will enable viewers to download and store programmes to view later. Once accessed, they will have seven days to view them.

Channel 4 became the first major commercial broadcaster to begin simulcasting all programmes it commissions on the internet and the move signalled the first step by the major broadcasters into the broadband TV, video-on-demand (VOD) and mobile world.

Under the agreement television advertisers are granted free 'airtime' on the internet and registered viewers are allowed free content. For the broadcasters, the PACT arrangement allows them to secure windows for the exploitation of new media rights in return for production firms making major gains in terms of control of their programmes. However, some commentators feel that the fact that PACT was threatening to usurp the traditional role of broadcasters – and forge direct relationships with non-traditional media platforms – undoubtedly helped.

The introduction of the agreement has removed one of the major stumbling blocks for the expansion of television companies into new services. However, there remains a question mark over what their business models will be and how they will make these moves pay.

Channel 4 is airing the same commercials that appear on television but does not charge television advertisers, extra taking the view that no currency currently exists. However, it is felt that many broadcasters will ultimately monetise even the early adopters of broadband television with a roll-out of a much wider video-on-demand service planned. The channel launched pay-per-view services for two major shows in a partnership with Disney. It is now looking into similar deals, as well as a major cross-platform roll-out of on-demand films under the FilmFour banner. Yet the bulk of its services are likely to remain free.

The BBC and ITV are also planning their own video-on-demand service via the BBC Media Player.

It is inevitable that advertisers will eventually be drawn into the world of video-on-demand and other new services and will increasingly be dealing not just with broadcasters, but also with production companies, in forging the deals.

The advertising industry was notoriously slow to take going online seriously. It now appears to be having the same problem working out how to make the most of its new content.

CHECKLIST

- Ensure that the film company understands its obligations under the Advertising Standards Authority Code and that the Code applies to internet-based promotions.

- Pay particular attention to the rules for advertising to children.

- Consider the rules relating to ringtone sales.

CHAPTER 13

Electronic Signatures and Online Film Sales

INTRODUCTION

As we noted in Chapter 2, it is possible to form a legally binding contract by simple exchange of e-mail. The parties would usually accept that the individuals who sent the messages were who they purported to be and that they had necessary authority to enter into the contract. However, as online business develops there are higher value deals being struck and these should not on any view be conducted on the basis of e-mail correspondence. They should be concluded based on properly drafted legal agreements reflecting the nature of the deal. If, for example, the film company were to require those who it wished to agree terms with to sign a contract online, the question arises of how this can be achieved. The real objective in having someone sign a document is to bind them or their organisation to the terms of the agreement. In the physical world one can see the person or even verify their signature on a fax document. It is reasonable not to assume that the signature is forged. With the internet it is more difficult to guarantee the authenticity of the person with whom a contract is to be concluded. For this reason in recent years electronic signatures which provide that authenticity have developed. Conducting business using electronic signatures requires a different mindset to conventional contract management because there are different risks.

In this chapter we will examine how the identity of a party to an online commercial contract can be authenticated using electronic signatures. It is fair to say that at the time of writing electronic signatures have not been widely adopted by industry at large. The market for such devices has not yet developed. However, they exist and can be utilised and so a brief review is warranted.

As we have seen with much of the law examined in this book, it is the European Union which dominates the legal regime to which online business is subject. In December 1999 the European Commission adopted the *Electronic Signatures Directive* as a response to the development of legislation by each member state. The main thrust of the legislation is twofold. First it imposes a requirement on each member state to provide for the legal recognition of electronic signatures. Second, it provides mutual recognition.

Before we examine the new legal framework which governs electronic signatures it is helpful to view it in its proper full legal context.

FORGERY

What do we refer to when we talk of forgery? Forgery of one's signature is a risk, albeit modest, which all of us face in everyday life and in business. The forgery usually occurs as a prior step to the commission of some other crime, most often a crime of deception, which will result in some material advantage (most obviously money or other property) to the forger.

In the UK, under English Law forgery and counterfeiting are regulated by the Forgery and Counterfeiting Act 1981.

THE DEFINITION OF FORGERY

A person is guilty of forgery if he of she makes a 'false instrument' and for this purpose 'instrument' is defined by Section 8 of the Act:

> 'instrument' means
>
> (a)   ... any document, whether of a formal or informal character;
>
> (b)   ... any disk, tape, soundtrack or other device on or in which information is recorded or stored by mechanical, electronic or other means.

It can be seen that the internet can constitute an 'instrument' for the purposes of the statutory definition.

Section 9 of the Act states:

> (i)   an instrument is false for the purpose of this part of this Act:
>
> (a)   if it purports to have been made in the form in which it is made by a person who did not in fact make it in that form; or
>
> (b)   if it purports to have been made in the form in which it is on the authority of a person who did not in fact authorise its making in that form; or
>
> (c)   if it purports to have been made in the terms in which it is made by the person who did not in fact make it in those terms; or

(d)   *if it purports to have made in the terms in which it is made on the authority who did not in fact authorise its making in those terms; or ...*

(h)   *if it purports to have been made or altered by an existing person but he did not in fact exist.*

(ii)   *a person is to be treated ... as making a false instrument if he alters an instrument so as to make it false in any respect ....*

THE FORM OF AN ELECTRONIC SIGNATURE

The term 'electronic signature' actually covers many forms of electronic technology. It can even be a retinal scan to verify personal identity. As will be seen in this section, the law recognises the rapid pace of development and has attempted to legislate the use of electronic signatures in a technology-neutral fashion. In other words, for the purpose of drafting laws which will govern for many years to come, the law does not simple assume the existence of only one form of electronic signature. For present purposes we will refer to the most commonly understood and thus far utilised form of electronic signature in industry. In effect, the electronic signature is a stamp which appears as an icon and which can be attached to an electronic document. Its appearance and application is straightforward. Its underlying technology is not. It relies on cryptography.

Cryptography as a method of sending the contents of a message has been used from ancient times. In the context of the internet, cryptography is the science of keeping communications private. Cryptography has long been applied by banks and is an essential tool for electronic commerce. It can be used as the basis of an electronic signature or to keep electronic data confidential. It also ensures that the integrity of such information is preserved. A central element of cryptography is encryption, which is the transformation of data into an intelligible form.

Encryption is the process by which a message is disguised sufficiently to hide the substance of the content. It involves turning normal text into a series of letters and/or numbers which can only be deciphered by someone who has the correct password or key. Encryption is used to prevent others from reading confidential, private or commercial data, for example, an e-mail sent over the internet.

In essence, contemporary cryptographic search systems change readable symbols into a second set of unreadable symbols using a mathematical process controlled by a number. This number is called a key.

The following indicates a process:

> film production company A writes to film distributor B 'We agree your terms';

> the message is encrypted as follows:

> '196421043520418N620181727227'

To read the message, film distributor B must know how the message was encrypted. If they know the key to the unreadable symbols they can work out the message when they receive it. This example does not adequately demonstrate the use of a mathematical formula, but is intended to illustrate how the concept works. There are two types of mathematical families that permit the message to be disguised.

Encryption technology therefore provides the ability to create and validate electronic signatures through the use of what is called 'asynchronous' or 'public key' cryptography. The system uses two keys to encrypt and decrypt a message. It is this feature that is used for signatures.

By use of this process a document can be signed using one's private key. Anyone can then use the corresponding public key to verify the identity of the signatory as only their private key will correspond. However, of itself that process cannot identify and verify the owner or holder of the private key. To do that a trusted third party arrangement is necessary.

CERTIFICATION AUTHORITIES

Certification Authorities or trusted third parties are public or private bodies that certify the connection between a person and their public key number. The Certification Authority guarantees the authenticity of the public key number.

Put simply, the trusted third party certifies that, to the best of its knowledge, the identity of the signature holder is that which is claimed. The Certification Authority issues an 'electronic authentication certificate' which has the following characteristics:

- it identifies the Certification Authority;
- it identifies the subscriber;

- it contains the subscriber's public key;

- it is digitally signed with the Certification Authority's private key.

The electronic authentication certificate also contains other information, such as the level of enquiry carried out by the Certification Authority before issuing the certificate.

It is necessary for the film company to provide the Certification Authority with a copy of the public key number and proof of identify, together with sufficient credentials to demonstrate an authority to deal with high value transactions. When film production company A sends a message to film distributor B, it also sends film distributor B a copy of its Certificate. Film distributor B's computer will decrypt the message according to the key they have been given. At the same time, the Certification Authority will confirm to film distributor B that:

a)   film production company A is who it purports to be;

b)   the certificate has not been revoked nor has it expired.

In summary, the role of Certification Authorities, is to provide certificates that establish the identity of the owner of the public key number.

THE ELECTRONIC COMMUNICATIONS ACT 2000

In 2000 the UK government introduced the Electronic Communications Act. The main purpose of the Act is to help build confidence in electronic commerce and its underlying technology. The Act was in fact the first piece of UK legislation written specifically for the internet. First, it provides an approval scheme for businesses and other organisations providing cryptography services, such as electronic signature, services and confidentiality services. Second, it gives legal recognition of electronic signatures and third, it removes obstacles in other legislation to the use of electronic communications and storage in place of paper.

The Act is in three parts:

Part I – Cryptography Service Providers

This concerns the arrangements for registering providers of cryptography support services, such as electronic signature services and confidentiality services.

Part II – Facilitation of Electronic Commerce, Data Storage, etc.

This part of the Act makes provision for the legal recognition of electronic signatures. It will also facilitate the use of electronic communications or electronic storage of information, as an alternative to traditional means of communication or storage.

Part III – Miscellaneous and Supplemental

This part of the legislation is concerned with the modification of telecommunication licences, including territorial extent of the Act.

For the purposes of this book we shall consider Parts I and II of the Act.

PART I – CRYPTOGRAPHY SERVICE PROVIDERS

The Act creates a register of approved providers. Section I places a duty on the Secretary of State to establish and maintain a register of approved providers of cryptography support services and specifies what information is contained in the register. The public have right of access to the register and any changes to it must be publicised.

The idea behind the register is that it will be voluntary but will promote minimum standards of quality and service to be met in relation to cryptography support services. The government has indicated that if the self-regulatory scheme works there will be no need to set up a statutory scheme.

The provisions in the Act relating to the establishment of the statutory scheme are subject to a 'sunset clause'. This states that if a statutory scheme has not been set up within five years then the government's power to set one up will lapse.

Cryptography support services include:

- confidentiality – in other words, securing that such electronic communications or data can be accessed or put into an intelligible form, that is, restored to the condition which it was before any encryption or similar process was applied to it, only by certain persons;

- ensuring, by use of an electronic signature, that the authenticity or integrity of electronic communications or data is capable of being ascertained;

- registration and certification in relation to certificates, time stamping of certificates or documents, key generation and management, key storage and providing directories of certificates.

The Act makes clear that the approval scheme for cryptography support services only includes those services which primarily involve a continuing relationship between the supplier of the service and a customer.

PART II – FACILITATION OF ELECTRONIC COMMERCE

Perhaps the most obvious change the Act makes is that it provides for the admissibility of electronic signatures and related certificates in legal proceedings, that is, in court.

Section 7(2) Electronic Communications Act 2000 defines Digital signatures as:

> *Anything in electronic form as … is incorporated into or otherwise logically associated with any electronic communication or electronic data and purports to be so incorporated or associated for the purpose of being used in establishing the authenticity of the communication as data in the integrity of the communication or data, or both.*

The courts will decide on this question of authentication or integrity of a message in the event of dispute. In addition it is possible for a film company to contract with another business on how their respective electronic signatures are to be treated.

An electronic signature can be used as evidence of authenticity or integrity in court proceedings. Section 7(1) allows an electronic signature or its certification, to be admissible as evidence on this question.

There are three elements to establishing authenticity of an electronic communication. First, whether the communication or data comes from a particular person or other source; second, whether it is accurately timed and dated; and third, whether it is intended to have legal effect. One concern raised during the government's consultation period highlights this issue. The outdated definitions of words such as 'writing' and 'signature' in law were significant barriers to the development of electronic commerce in this country.

In Clause 8 the Act includes a power to enable ministers to draw up secondary legislation to permit such requirements to be met electronically. For example, the Department of Trade and Industry used powers under the

Act to amend the Companies Act 1985 to enable companies to communicate with shareholders electronically. Large music businesses can now send out of meetings and other matters required under the Companies Act notifications to shareholders by e-mail rather than post: a useful ability. when there are thousands of shareholders.

CHECKLIST

- Be aware that an electronic signature has the same legal effect as a physical signature.

- Ensure that the film company understands how electronic signatures operate with the use of Certification Authorities.

CHAPTER 14

Disability Discrimination Issues for Film and Television Websites

THE DISABILITY DISCRIMINATION ACT 1995 AND WEB ACCESSIBILITY BEST PRACTICE

It is important to appreciate that the Disability Discrimination Act 1995 has been in force for over 12 years. When it was introduced it did not contemplate the internet – and specifically websites – as falling within its ambit. At that time, whilst those in the new media sector were well aware of the internet and its commercial potential, legislators were not.

In essence the Act makes it unlawful for a service provider to discriminate against a disabled person by refusing to provide any service that it provides to members of the public. A service provider would include a website development company and most likely a film company which operates as website.

In 2004 the Disability Rights Commission in the United Kingdom launched an investigation into 1,000 websites, of which over 80 per cent were next to impossible for disabled people to use. They warned firms they could face legal action under the Disability Discrimination Act. However, in most cases where a website is found to be in breach the DRC would warn the website operator first rather than simply go ahead and sue. Therefore, legal action would probably not be pursued as the website would be corrected following the warning.

The internet governing body is the W3C. It is widely believed that, if a case comes before the courts, the W3C accessibility guidelines will be used to assess a website's accessibility and decide the outcome of the case. The W3C offers levels of compliance. Priority 1 guidelines, which must be satisfied according to the W3C, and Priority 2 guidelines, which should be satisfied and are the European Union recommended level of compliance.

In 2004 the Disability Rights Commission prepared a report based on their investigation of websites. The report is not law but it is a useful guide to the kind of problems faced by disabled or impaired people as regards websites. At the time of writing there are no reported legal cases on breach of accessibility.

The impairment groups represented in the user testing for the report were:

- blind people who use screen readers with synthetic speech or Braille output;

- partially sighted people who may use screen magnification;

- people who are profoundly deaf and hard of hearing;

- people with specific learning difficulties such as dyslexia;

- physically impaired people whose use of the web may be affected by their lack of control of arms and hands, by tremor and by lack of dexterity in hands and fingers.

The report makes a number of recommendations to improve the position, including the following:

- website commissioners should formulate written policies for meeting the needs of disabled people. This might include ensuring that disabled people with a range of sensory, cognitive and mobility impairments are involved from early in the process of website design and development;

- those who provide and oversee education and training of web developers, including those who sell web-authoring tools, should promote an understanding that good practice entails attending and responding to the needs of disabled people. This might include ensuring that modules form an integral part of any continuing professional development or product support;

- web designers themselves should accept that good practice entails attending and responding to the needs of disabled people. This would involve taking steps to familiarise themselves with how disabled people use the web and with their needs in web accessibility;

- the government should raise awareness, for example, by publicity campaigns aimed at web designers and commissioners;

- website designers should involve disabled people in the design and testing of websites at an early stage;

- web designers should not rely exclusively on automated accessibility training;

- developers of automated accessibility checking tools should enhance their functionality to make them more useful to website commissioners and website developers;

- the designers and providers of assistive technology should enable and encourage users to keep their products up to date.

It is helpful to consider the key problems experienced by impairment groups according to the Disability Rights Commission report findings. Such a review will assist the film company in properly developing its website to ensure that it meets Disability Guidelines. The report did not concentrate on film websites but rather websites across a range of activities.

BLIND USERS

- Incompatibility between screen-reading software and webpages, for example, the assistive technology not detecting some links or its proving impossible to highlight text using text-to-speech software.

- Incorrect or non-existent labelling of links, form elements and frames.

- Cluttered and complex page structures.

- ALT tags on images non-existent or unhelpful.

- Confusing and disorienting navigation mechanisms.

PARTIALLY-SIGHTED USERS

- Inappropriate use of colours and poor contrast between content and background.

- Incompatibility between accessibility software, for example, for magnification and webpages.

- Unclear and confusing layout of pages.

- Graphics and text too small.

- Confusing and disorienting navigation mechanisms.

PHYSICALLY IMPAIRED USERS

- Confusing and disorienting navigation mechanisms.

- Unclear and confusing layout of pages.

- Graphics and text size too small.

- Inappropriate use of colours and poor contrast between content and background.

HEARING-IMPAIRED USERS

- Unclear and confusing layout of pages.

- Confusing and disorienting navigation mechanisms.

- Lack of alternative media for audio-based information and complex terms/language.

- Inappropriate use of colours and poor contrast between content and background.

- Graphics and text too small.

DYSLEXIC USERS

- Unclear and confusing layout of pages.

- Confusing and disorienting navigation mechanisms.

- Inappropriate use of colours and poor contrast between content and background.

- Graphics and text too small.

- Complicated language and terminology.

There any other pointers for the film company to adopt best practice in its website. These include:

- provide a text equivalent for every non-text element;

- ensure foreground and background colour combinations provide sufficient contrast when viewed by someone having colour deficits or when viewed on a black and white screen;

- until user agents allow users to freeze moving content, avoid movement in pages;

- divide large blocks of information into more manageable groups where natural and appropriate;

- clearly identify the target of each link;

- use the clearest and simplest language appropriate for a website's content.

CHAPTER 15

Whose Law Applies to Internet Film Sales?

BACKGROUND

It is easy to overlook the obvious fact that the internet is a global medium, which means that a website is available for view from anywhere in the world. In many instances the film company might not really be targeting its titles or merchandise at jurisdictions across the globe. It might wish to limit its online activity to the UK only. A number of websites operated by film companies are tailored for a given geographical territory. However, it is also common for film websites to make merchandise or services available to international visitors to the website. At first sight it might not appear obvious why we have to consider questions of legal jurisdiction in the context of online film distribution. As will be seen, it is, however, vital for any film company contemplating commercial internet activity to appreciate the impact that legal jurisdiction will have on its business.

A contract formed online has the potential to produce transnational disputes between the parties. We have seen in Chapter 3 that a film company would usually state in its website terms and conditions that English law will govern its online contract. Whilst this is a vital inclusion, there are certain instances when supplying merchandise or services via the internet from the European Union where strict rules must be followed.

It is important for a film company to understand with certainty where it can be sued and where it can take legal action. When we refer to the question of whose law applies to internet film sales we are really considering two issues: first, the jurisdiction or country in which a dispute will be heard; and second, whose set of laws will apply to that dispute, regardless of where the trial is held. The English courts are required to follow certain rules on jurisdiction and choice of law. This is the issue to be examined in this chapter.

THE BRUSSELS REGULATION 2001

On 1 March 2002 the *Brussels Regulation on Jurisdiction and the Enforcement on Judgements in Civil and Commercial Matters (2001 OJ L012,16.01.2001)* was introduced. The Regulations replaced the former Brussels Convention. It is necessary to start by establishing whether the Regulation applies.

We will consider first the question of the proper jurisdiction. This issue relates to in which country the film company that operates a website can be sued and indeed take legal action. A vital issue is where the defendant to a commercial dispute is 'domiciled'. This is because, under the Brussels Regulation, someone domiciled in an EU member state can be sued in the courts of that state. So, for example, if a UK film company finds that the copyright in its website is being infringed by a German company, the UK business can sue the infringer in the German courts. This concept of domicile also applies to contracts formed over the internet. Clearly, if a film company were to sue another business for copyright infringement or indeed any other matter, the defendant would either be domiciled in a member state or a non-member state. If domicile lies within a member state, the Brussels Regulation rules will apply. If the defendant is domiciled outside a member state (anywhere else in the world), other legal rules prevail.

It is necessary to make a distinction between an individual who is domiciled in a country and a company so domiciled.

INDIVIDUAL DOMICILE

In the case of an individual, that person is deemed domiciled within the United Kingdom only if they are resident in the UK and it can be shown that the individual has a substantial connection with the UK. That will depend on the nature and circumstances of his or her residence. However, there is a presumption that being resident for the previous three months or more will constitute this 'substantial connection'.

If an individual is not deemed to be domiciled in the United Kingdom for the purposes of the Brussels Regulation, it is necessary to then establish if the individual is domiciled within another EU state. If that person is not regarded as being domiciled within the EU, then the Brussels Regulation will have no bearing on the commercial dispute.

There is a simple test that must be applied to establish if an individual is in fact domiciled in another EU member state, which is whether the other state would regard the individual as domiciled there. The Brussels Regulation prescribes that the persons domiciled must be assessed from the particular state's legal perspective.

If the individual is not domiciled in any EU member state the test is twofold. First, the individual must be resident in that non-EU country. Second, the nature and circumstances of residence must indicate that the individual has a substantial connection with that country.

CORPORATE DOMICILE

The Brussels Regulation makes it clear that a company or other legal person is to be regarded as domiciled in the state where it has its statutory seat, central administration, or principal place of business.

To establish whether a company is domiciled in the UK, the test to apply is as follows. If the company or other legal person was incorporated or formed under a law which is part of the UK and its registered office or other official address is in the UK, or if its central administration or principal place of business is in the UK, then UK domicile will be established.

A frequently asked question in the context of internet-related disputes is whether a company which is based in the UK can avoid the jurisdiction of the English courts simply by using a server offshore. The answer is that it cannot. The ownership, control or access to a website in the world is irrelevant to the principle of jurisdiction under the Brussels Regulation.

Having established that a company or other legal person is not domiciled in the UK for the purpose of the Brussels Regulation, it is necessary to settle whether domicile lies in another EU state. The Brussels Regulation will not apply to a commercial dispute if the company or organisation is not domiciled within the EU.

Once again there are two tests to establish if a company or organisation is domiciled in the EU though not in the UK. In the first instance the English courts must be satisfied that the company or other legal person was formed or incorporated under the law of that other EU state, or alternatively, that its central management and control is exercised in that EU state. The corporate entity must not have been formed under the law of any part of the UK or shown to be regarded by the courts of the EU country to have its seat within an EU state.

If these various tests do not establish that the defendant in a commercial dispute is domiciled either in the UK or another EU member state, then the Brussels Regulation will not apply.

Once it has been determined where the defendant is domiciled, the defendant in a commercial dispute may be sued in the courts of his, her or its domicile or in the courts for the place of performance of the obligation in question. There are certain exceptions to this rule which are not relevant for our purposes, but one exception which does relate is if the contract has a specific jurisdiction clause.

SALE OF GOODS OR SUPPLY OF SERVICES CONTRACTS

Where goods are sold or services supplied there are two presumptions applied as to the place of performance of those contracts, unless it has been agreed otherwise. So, for example, where film merchandise is sold over the internet to a consumer, the relevant court is in the member state where the merchandise was or should have been delivered. The same approach applies to contracts for the supply of services. That is, the relevant court is the one in the EU country where the services were or should have been provided. If these presumptions do not apply, it is necessary to establish where a place of performance of the obligation was.

The most important point to stress is that if a film company operates a website from within the EU it is vital to include a jurisdiction clause in the online contract if the principal obligations are to be performed outside the home state of the film company.

ARTICLE 15(I) BRUSSELS REGULATION

It is important to note that all EU-based consumers can sue either in the member state the consumer resides in or in the courts for the member state in which the film company is based. Proceedings may be brought against a consumer by a film company only in the courts of the member state in which the consumer is domiciled. Thus, a UK-based film company operating online may find itself being drawn into litigation away from the UK. This would be a problem not least because the film company would have to instruct a UK lawyer who in turn would need to instruct a lawyer qualified in the particular jurisdiction. Whilst some international law firms might have offices based in that jurisdiction, the professional fees of such transnational disputes can be considerable.

One might think that the issue of proper jurisdiction when dealing with consumers is straightforward. Certainly it is clear enough that the Brussels Regulation provides protection to consumers in relation to consumer contracts. Article 15(i) of the Regulation defines a 'consumer contract' as one which can be regarded as being outside the consumer's trade or profession where the contract:

a)   is for the sale of goods on instalment credit terms or;

b)   is a loan repayment by instalments, or for any other form of credit made to finance the sale of goods or;

c)   has, in all other cases, been concluded by the person who pursues commercial or professional activities in the member state of the consumer's domicile, or by any means, directs such activities to that member state or the several states including that member state and the contract falls within the scope of such activities.

It is the category of contract at Article 15(i)(c) above which causes difficulties with internet activities. There are two situations where activity might be 'directed' to a member state and hence invoke the protection in favour of the consumer of the Brussels Regulation.

First, the Regulation will apply where the internet film company pursues its commercial activities in the consumer's member state and the contract falls within the scope of such activities. For example, the activity of the film company might be to sell film DVDs to consumers in France. If the contract at issue involved the online sales of such DVDs to French consumers, the Regulation will apply.

The second scenario where the Brussels Regulation will apply is where the film company by any means directs its commercial activities to the member state of the consumer domicile, or to several states, including that member state, and the contract falls within the scope of such activities. This is a complex area of law and needs to be examined in more detail.

If the online film company pursues commercial activity in the consumer's member state the position is as follows.

Here, the contract being sued upon must fall within the scope of the activities being pursued in the member state of the consumer's domicile. However, the Brussels Regulations have an additional requirement. This pursuit of the activity within the consumer's member state must also relate to the consumer's contract under dispute. It is not enough for a film company, for example, to target its activities at a particular EU member state of the consumer's residence or at a number of member states which included that member state. The contract must also be concluded within the framework of its activities. It is necessary, therefore, for a film company to consider all of its activities within each particular member state of concern. It will be necessary for the film company to be certain that any contracts it enters into with EU consumers in that member state are not related to any other commercial or professional activities pursued in those member states.

Article 15(i)(c) becomes even more difficult in its application when one considers a second situation in which it might apply. This is where the supplier 'by any means' directs commercial or professional activities to the member state of the consumer's domicile. When considering this Article in the context of internet activity, whether the internet is accessed by the consumer via PC or mobile apparatus, the question is, when is a website 'directed' to a member state?

The courts will be required to decide on this test on a case-by-case basis. However, it is clear that an internet website simply being accessible is not sufficient for Article 15 to be applicable. Two factors which will be relevant is if the website solicits the conclusion of distance contracts (see Chapter 8) and whether a contract has actually been concluded at a distance. In such circumstances it is possible to argue that the film website is being 'directed' towards particular consumers in the EU.

One issue to note is that the language or monetary currency which the film company website uses is not relevant for the purpose of the test of 'directing activity'. It is thus the actual conduct of the film company in the particular member state that determines whether or not activities are in fact directed to that member state.

It is helpful to consider some examples to illustrate the operation of the Brussels Regulation. If an Italian consumer cannot transact with a German film company website, but nonetheless still views it, it is clear that the German film company's commercial activity will not be held to be 'directed' at Italy. This would be the position even were the website presented in Italian.

In the UK, the Department of Trade and Industry have confirmed that to establish whether a website falls within Article 15(i)(c) it is necessary to look at the nature of that website. The UK approach is based on the following. The simple fact that a transaction can take place via the website in, for example, France does not mean that the website has been 'directed' at France. The determining factor is the 'nature' of the website. It can be seen that this issue is susceptible to controversy and it is likely to give rise to disputes on the applicability of the Brussels Regulation to a particular business activity of a film company offered online.

The importance of internet terms and conditions on a film company website is clearly paramount. It would also be wise for the film company for example based in the UK to specify on its website a menu of EU Countries which are specifically excluded from its online activity. In addition, the technical formatting of the website itself by the use of geo-filtering technology (see Chapter 5, p. 49) might permit the shielding of consumers from a particular country although this of itself might not guarantee suitable exclusion.

THE CHOICE OF LAW

We have considered above the question of the proper legal jurisdiction and the effect of the Brussels Regulation. That issue related to which country the film website operator can be sued and take legal action.

The next issue to consider is the actual choice of law, for example, will it be English, French, or a particular US state law? It is inevitable that the internet will permit an increasing number of contracts to be formed between parties from a variety of legal jurisdictions

THE ROME CONVENTION

The Rome Convention permits a choice of which law can govern a contract. The Convention applies throughout the EU, but in the UK it is incorporated into the *Contracts (Applicable Law) Act 1990*. The Convention applies to all contracts made after 1 April 1991.

There are two forms of contract which can be made over the internet for the purpose of the Rome Convention:

1 where the contract actually specifies the law that will govern the contract and this is agreed; and

2 where the law that will govern the contract between the parties has not been agreed.

Any UK commercial activity conducted over the internet should, as a matter of course, include an applicable law clause in the internet terms and conditions (see Chapter 3).

The Rome Convention makes it clear that a choice of law can be expressed, as in the case where the website terms and conditions make clear those laws which will govern the online contract. It should be noted that a choice of law can be expressed even though it is not actually specified in the contract. It may instead be demonstrated by the terms of the contract or the particular circumstances of the case. Therefore, an express choice of law may be deemed to have been made even where the contract does not specify, for example, that English law will govern. This demonstration of choice in the absence of a clear statement depends entirely on the facts in each case. These facts may be open to interpretation and thus uncertainty in the context of internet transactions across borders and so specific legal advice must always be taken when a film company establishes its international website operations.

There are circumstances where these express choice of law rules are varied. Article 5(2) of the Rome Convention makes clear that in certain circumstances, even though a choice of law is made by the parties to an online contract, a consumer may still benefit from the laws of his or her country of habitual residence. Since the internet permits global transactions, the effect of Article 5 is significant. This overriding of the usual position applies, for example, if in that country the conclusion of the contract was preceded by a specific invitation addressed to the consumer or by advertising and the consumer in that country had taken all the steps necessary on his or her part for the conclusion of the contract.

This can cause problems with internet contracts, because a website may be regarded as a form of advertising. If a film website does not actually block viewers from specified countries, as outlined above, there is a risk that consumer protection laws may be introduced into a contract which the film company website operator never intended. Both the Rome Convention and the Brussels Regulation clearly protect consumers who contract with websites that make no attempt to exclude them.

CHECKLIST

- If the film company website is intended to be accessed by an international audience, ensure that the company understands the impact of the Brussels Regulation and Rome Convention.

- Review the film company website terms and conditions to ensure they address fully the question of sales of merchandise to European-based consumers.

CHAPTER 16

The Audiovisual Media Services Directive

BACKGROUND

The Television Without Frontiers Directive (89/552/EEC) was adopted on 3 October 1989 by the European Council and amended on 30 June 1997 by the European Parliament and the Council Directive 97/36/EC. The Directive established the legal framework for the free movement of television broadcasting services in the European Union to promote the development of a European market in broadcasting and related activities such as television advertising. So, if a broadcaster is licensed in one member state they are free to broadcast in another country in the European Union without the need for further licensing. It was designed to avoid the prospect of multiple regulations because there would only be one country of origin. The Directive harmonises the law regarding the television broadcasting activities of its member states. The Directive addresses issues which include the free movement of programmes within the EU, advertising and sponsorship provisions and threshold windows of television exploitation for feature films.

The Directive is now the subject of a second revision. The reason is that, with the rapid development of technology in the last few years, it has very quickly become dated. Communication technology has transformed the way in which broadcast transmissions can be accessed and in particular the internet opens up new vistas for content distribution. In an age when television can be delivered to a mobile phone, the European Commission decided to launch a review of the original Directive to accommodate new technology.

The latest incarnation, which is due to replace the 1997 law, reflects the advance of the internet, mobile telephones and the switch from analogue to digital TV technologies.

The European Commission published its proposal for the revision of the Television Without Frontiers (TVWF) Directive on 13 December 2005. The proposal extends the scope of the Directive to on-demand and online services which are together described as non-linear services with a lower level of controls and regulation than applies to traditional television broadcasting or linear services. The title was also changed to 'Audiovisual Media Services Directive'.

In essence, the proposed changes relate to changes to the country of origin provisions and the relaxation of some provisions relating to the amount and frequency of advertising on television. Further, it proposed that product placement in programmes should be explicitly permitted, subject to certain conditions relating to editorial integrity and notification to viewers of the presence of product placement.

The government sought consultation with the television industry, new media service providers, trade unions and civil society organisations on 6 June 2006.[1] Contributors to the consultation included the BBC, BT plc, Direct Marketing Association, Confederation of British Industry, British Screen Advisory Panel, ITV, Channels 4 and Five and the Internet Service Providers Association. There were a number of options available with regard to the original Directive and upon which the industry was canvassed:

1   repeal the Directive;

2   make no changes to the Directive;

3   focus the amendments and clarify the text to make the advertising rules more flexible and ensure that the Directive covered all those linear services which were similar to television.

4   amend the Directive to cover both linear and non-linear services subject only to the basic tier of rules.

5   amend the Directive to cover both linear and non-linear services, but with both the basic tier and also the more detailed linear rules about the coverage of major events, quotas of European and independently produced programming and advertising rights of reply applying to the two types of service.

At the time of writing, discussions on the revision of the Directive are continuing in the Council of Ministers and the European Parliament. The Parliament is expected to adopt its first reading opinion leading to a response by the Council in Spring 2007. The proposal as revised will then be subject to a second reading in the Parliament and the Council. A final text is not expected to be adopted until late 2007 or early 2008.

---

1   Department for Culture, Media and Sport Consultation on the proposal by the European Commission for the revision of the Television Without Frontiers Directive, Report, December 2006.

A REVIEW OF THE AUDIOVISUAL SERVICES DIRECTIVE PRIMARY PROVISIONS

PURPOSE

The proposed Directive acknowledges that new technologies in the transmission of audiovisual media services call for adaptation of the regulatory framework to take account of the impact of structural change, the spread of information and communication technologies (ICT) and technological developments on business models. The Directive is intended to ensure optimal conditions of competitiveness and legal certainty for Europe's information technologies and its media industries and services, as well as respect for cultural and linguistic diversity.

The proposals state that the laws, regulations and administrative measures should be as unobtrusive and simple as possible to allow new and existing audiovisual media services to develop and flourish, thus allowing for job creation, economic growth, innovation and cultural diversity to be nurtured.

The European Parliament considers that audiovisual media services are as much cultural goods as they are economic goods. Their growing importance for societies, democracy – in particular by ensuring freedom of information, diversity of opinion and media pluralism – education and culture justifies the application of specific rules to these services and the enforcement of those rules, notably in order to preserve the fundamental rights and freedoms laid down in the Charter of Fundamental Rights of the European Union, the European Convention for Protection of Human Rights and Fundamental Freedoms and the United Nations Covenant on Civil and Political Freedoms, and in order to ensure the protection of minors and vulnerable and disabled people.

Traditional audiovisual media services such as television and emerging on-demand audiovisual media services offer significant employment opportunities in the European Community, particularly in small and medium-sized enterprises, and stimulate economic growth and investment. Bearing in mind the importance of a level playing-field and a true European broadcasting market, the basic principles of the common market, such as competition law and equal treatment, should be respected in order to ensure transparency and predictability in media markets and to achieve low entry barriers.

Legal uncertainty and an uneven playing field exist for European companies delivering audiovisual media services as regards the legal regime governing emerging on-demand services. In order to avoid distortions of competition, it is therefore necessary to improve legal certainty, help complete the internal market and facilitate the emergence of a single information area which can apply to all audiovisual media services, both linear and non-linear, irrespective of whether they are transmitted on the basis of a set programme schedule or on demand. The proposed Directive intends to provide at least a basic tier of coordinated rules aimed at guaranteeing a sufficient level of protection of children, the vulnerable and the disabled and respect for fundamental rights and freedoms.

AUDIOVISUAL SERVICES COVERED BY THE PROPOSED DIRECTIVE

The definition of audiovisual media services covers all audiovisual mass-media services whose content is suitable for television broadcasting, irrespective of the delivery platform. This includes whether the editorial approach and responsibility of the provider are reflected in a programme schedule or in a selection catalogue. However, its scope is limited to services covering any form of economic activity, including that of public service enterprises. The economic element must be significant to justify the application of the Directive. Economic activities are normally provided for remuneration, intended for a certain period and characterised by a certain continuity. The assessment of the economic element is subject to the criteria and rules of the country of origin. Accordingly, the definition of audiovisual media services does not cover non-economic activities not normally provided for remuneration, such as weblogs and other user-generated content, or any form of private correspondence, such as e-mails and private websites.

The definition of audiovisual media services covers the exercise of editorial responsibility by mass media in their function to inform, entertain and educate the general public. It includes audiovisual commercial communications but excludes any form of private correspondence, such as e-mails sent to a limited number of recipients. The definition also excludes all services whose principal purpose is not the distribution of audiovisual content, that is, where any audiovisual content is merely incidental to the service. Examples include websites that contain audiovisual elements only in an ancillary manner, such as animated graphical elements, small advertising spots or information related to a product or non-audiovisual service. It also excludes games of chance involving a stake representing a sum of money, including lotteries and betting, provided that their main purpose is not that of distributing audiovisual content. Further examples are online games and search engines, as long as the principal purpose of the audiovisual media service is not fulfilled.

Television broadcasting services, that is, linear services, currently include in particular analogue and digital television, live streaming, webcasting and near-video-on-demand. By contrast, video-on-demand, for example, is one of the on-demand, that is, non-linear services. For linear audiovisual media services or television programmes which are also offered on a live or deferred basis as non-linear services by the same media service provider, the requirements of this Directive are deemed to be met by the linear transmission. However, where different kinds of services are offered in parallel, without one part being clearly subordinate to another, the Directive should still apply to those distinguishable parts of the service that fulfil all the criteria of an audiovisual media service.

It is important to note that the definitions in the proposed Directive – in particular the definitions of television broadcasting, linear and non-linear services – are laid down only for the purposes of the Directive and do not affect the underlying rights protected by copyright and neighbouring rights legislation. The scope and regime of these rights are not prejudiced by these definitions and continue to be regulated independently by the relevant legislation.

The proposed Directive does not cover electronic versions of newspapers and magazines. Games of chance are also excluded.

For the purposes of the proposed Directive, the term 'audiovisual' refers to moving images with or without sound, and so includes silent films but does not cover audio transmission or radio services.

An audiovisual media service consists of programmes, that is, a discrete succession of moving images with or without sound which are subject to editorial responsibility and are either transmitted by a media service provider in accordance with a set time schedule or arranged in a catalogue.

This notion of editorial responsibility is essential for defining the role of the media service provider and thereby for the definition of audiovisual media services. 'Editorial responsibility' means responsibility for the selection and organisation, on a professional basis, of the content of an audiovisual offer. This may apply to an individual content or a collection of contents. Such editorial responsibility applies to the composition of the schedule, in the case of television programmes, or to the programme listing, in the case of non-linear services.

PRACTICAL ISSUES FACED BY THE TELEVISION AND NEW MEDIA INDUSTRIES WITH REGARD TO THE AUDIOVISUAL SERVICES DIRECTIVE

It is useful to consider the proposals here because of the convergence of broadcast media and the increase in web-based transmission of film content. It is no longer necessary to employ complex and expensive equipment to broadcast to a wide audience and if a film business is considering web-based television services then it must understand the direction the law is headed.

It is helpful to review here the various concerns raised by the industry as a whole to aspects of the proposed new Directive. These arguments serve as useful data for the reader when considering the matter of new platforms in general and can help shape strategic thinking.

There are immediate problems that the regulators need to consider. For example, the traditional broadcast model sees content delivered at pre-determined time schedules via standard television sets. In effect, the programmes are 'pushed' to the viewer. However, with internet broadcasts the position is more complex. First, the content is available for access at the time of the user's choosing and thus the programmes are 'pulled' by the viewer when they want them. Second, there is far more variation in terms of what constitutes a programme with regard to what can be sent via the internet. The new rules being considered only cover commercial broadcasts but the regulators appear to be making the distinction between services controlled by the broadcast operator, or linear services, and those where the consumer chooses, or non-linear services. It is likely that detailed controls in terms of advertising will probably only apply to linear services and not, therefore, to a substantial amount of content which is delivered over the internet.

With an increasingly sophisticated array of delivery mechanisms further difficulties arise in drawing the line between linear and non-linear. There is going to be a range of 'hybrid' services where visual content is delivered using a combination of routes to the consumer.

There are some reservations about the practical effect of the new Directive. Content regulated in Europe would not have any impact on the vast majority of content providers who operate outside the EU. The rules might not work effectively for audiovisual websites hosted overseas which, of course, can be viewed in Europe. In addition, if regulation of internet broadcasts is introduced in Europe, there is a danger of a handover of commercial and legal advantage to content providers based elsewhere in the world.

LINEAR AND NON-LINEAR SERVICES

It is difficult to be precise about the distinction between linear and non-linear services as the sectors are currently converging. However, the following definitions appear to be acknowledged.

The definition of 'linear services' – television channels delivered via the traditional TV distribution methods – covers:

- TV channels specifically created for distribution on the internet. It is not clear how many of these channels are likely to emerge;

- TV channels specifically created for distribution on mobile phones. Many traditional broadcasters had created versions of their main TV channels with a schedule that included mainly their own productions and programming for which they hold rights for 3G distribution;

- near-video-on-demand services via satellite, which are between linear and non-linear services. The schedule is decided by the provider but the subscriber pays a fee per viewing. The fact that the provider offers a selection could bring the service closer to video-on-demand, but the prescheduled feature makes the service seem closer to linear services.

The definition of 'non-linear services' covers:

- video-on-demand over xDSL/IPTV;

- video-on-demand services over the internet;

- subscription video-on-demand services over xDSL/IPTV (the viewer pays a monthly fee rather than a fee per programme);

- Subscription video-on-demand services over the internet (the viewer pays a monthly fee rather than a fee per programme).

OVERLAPS BETWEEN THE SUB-SECTORS

Traditional broadcasters are keen to stream their programmes over the internet, but at the time of writing, clearance rights prevent them from doing so. Studios are reluctant to grant such rights because they are more interested in exploiting their programmes on the internet themselves, using their own services or partnership websites. There are also security considerations. In terms of subscription video-on-demand services, particularly where there was a low subscription fee, companies would compete directly with pay and basic TV linear channels.

For mobile content, while not all of the services would fall within the scope of the Directive, it is thought likely that many of the higher value services and those with the greatest growth potential would. If the Directive brought significant compliance costs to service providers, the most dynamic segment of the market – mainly small entrepreneurial companies seeking to provide an array of new services to consumers – would be hardest hit.

The Producers Alliance for Cinema and Television (PACT) believes that the independent production sector is growing year on year, with total turnover rising from around £1 billion in 2003 to more than £1.7 billion in 2006. Most of PACT's membership was involved in content creation primarily for television and film. However, more and more companies are diversifying across different genres and types of content as the sector matures and interactive media is a rapidly growing part of their businesses.

It is thought that the characteristics of the new media market are dominated by low barriers to market entry (and exit), low distribution costs and historically limited formal sector specific regulation. These factors have served to encourage innovation and entrepreneurship, which could see new products and services brought to market in a relatively short time frame. The growth of this business model and the transition from traditional media to new business models are driven by consumer demand and changes in consumer patterns. The absence of regulated market entry assists this change and promotes a dynamic and fast-moving market. The value chain for new media involves a far higher number of interdependent players than does more traditional media. These could be both large and small businesses, which in many cases will have grown with, and will continue to depend upon the success of, upstream new media service providers. Many outwardly successful new services remain relatively small nascent markets requiring ongoing development and investment in order to be sustainable and profitable in the longer term. The development of these business models will continue to rely on flexibility within a stable and predictable framework.

PRACTICAL AND COMMERCIAL ISSUES RAISED BY THE PROPOSED AUDIOVISUAL SERVICES DIRECTIVE

The Effect of Widening the Scope of the Television Without Frontiers Directive

The first question to be considered is to what extent would widening the scope of the Directive either ease market entry for new providers of audiovisual media services or make it more difficult.

Any Directive covering audiovisual media services needs to offer certainty and predictability for providers and incentives to invest and responsiveness and flexibility in the light of technological developments. There must also be appropriate information and protection for the consumer. Many in the industry feel that there should be no extension of the Directive. There is a concern that it could add unnecessary new cost burdens – including licensing, compliance and legal costs – to fledgling business ventures that already have a high investment risk. There is also concern that, in the absence of clear guidance on the nature of the services covered by the Directive, the proposed revisions could act to create legal uncertainty in the future which might act as an impediment to the growth of services.

More work is thought by some to be required to improve the definition of linear television broadcasting (regardless of platform). The UK Film Council commented that both industry and citizens would benefit from some extension of the scope of the Directive, for example, to include film-on-demand services, provided that the Directive included workable definitions and flexibility in the way the definitions are applied.

It was also noted that it is difficult to distinguish between linear and non-linear services. Set-top boxes and Internet Protocol Television (IPTV) mean that even though the media service provider decides on a schedule, the viewer decides when to view the content. This line between linear and non-linear is likely to blur further as IPTV platforms evolve and viewers become users – for example, accessing e-mail at the same time as watching the news.

There is general acceptance that the Directive should be extended as there is likely to be a significant expansion towards watching television through cellular handsets and broadband internet. It makes sense, therefore, to include on-demand audiovisual material over the internet and mobile phones within the scope of the Directive.

There is some concern that the proposed Directive risks consigning commercial broadcasters to the non-convergent world. Content is king and commercial broadcasters are in the business of creating product that will draw audiences and attract advertisers. This means that they too must be allowed to innovate and cannot be subjected to unfair discrimination.

Determination of Own Prices, Product Characteristics and Quality Standards

The next question posed to the television and new media industry in the consultation was to what extent would widening the scope of the Directive limits the freedom of firms active in the markets which are affected to determine their own prices, product characteristics and/or quality and standards, means of advertising the product and distribution channels?

It was observed that the online world remains highly fluid. In contrast to traditional broadcasting, the nature of online content sites and channels could mean that services might fall outside the Directive when conceived or launched, but then come under the regulations at a later point. This could limit companies' ability to develop new services because of additional compliance and reporting costs or restrictions on advertising and regulatory uncertainty. It is argued that it is unclear how a prohibition on interference with editorial independence or a ban on inclusion of promotional messages within an audiovisual media service would be applied in a world of interactive content where material can be combined in different windows on the same screen.

It has also been noted that, unless the Directive is changed, broadcasters would have to compete with providers of linear and non-linear services via the internet, while the latter would not have to comply with the same advertising rules. This would mean that revenue levels would soon become affected and this could lead to a reduction in programme quality and standards. In the long term a significant proportion of channel distribution will take place via IPTV and the internet. If television channels delivered over the internet do not have to comply with advertising rules, such channels could in the long run have greater advertising revenue than television channels delivered on TV sets. If television channels delivered over the internet do not have to comply with similar advertising rules, in the long term such channels could secure more significant levels of advertising revenue than TV channels delivered on TV sets.

Costs and Benefits

The next question which came under industry consideration was what the cost and benefits to the UK, both direct and indirect, might be across various audiovisual services.

The Mobile Broadband Group (MBG) commented that in this country consumers spend over £13 billion per annum on basic mobile telephony, with an increasing proportion of people owning more than one mobile telephone. The market for mobile content had grown from nothing to £1 billion (not all audiovisual) in a period of around five years and therefore has potential for further growth. Thus, regulation that entailed high compliance costs for small content providers would have a dampening effect on this market.

An increase in regulation is felt by many to result in higher compliance costs. For example, with online content creation, budgets were far lower than for television production and therefore additional compliance costs would be proportionately higher. New obligations and costs on the regulator could drive operators currently established in this country to relocate outside the UK and perhaps even outside the EU. It is also possible that new markets could be cut off at source. The Confederation of British Industry (CBI) commented that in the face of competition from low cost overseas rivals, UK businesses were developing higher value services and greater customer loyalty through building more sophisticated online services. A CBI survey conducted in 2005 showed that 68 per cent of companies engaged with their customers online, with increased investment in functions and applications such as customer relationship and information management systems. This compared with 50 per cent in 2002. Any change in the regulatory regime would presumably have a significant impact on this development.

Another concern is that revision of the Directive would curb innovative uses of the internet. The current proposals brought into question the ability to run social networking sites and the promotion of broadband-driven services such as music and video. It would prevent the introduction of new programmes which would probably be free to broadcast online and which do not make it through to traditional television. This would be to the detriment of both the producers and the consumers of such content. In addition, extending the regulations to content delivered over the internet would place additional unknown burdens on hosting providers who were likely to be liable for infringing content once they were made aware of it.

One positive aspect of the proposed changes which is acknowledged by the industry as a whole is the creation of a level playing field that would force those audiovisual services operators who were unwilling or unable to comply with the regulatory obligations to move out of the UK. It is recognised, however, that such companies might simply establish their operations outside this country while still continuing to target UK viewers.

It is clear to anyone who uses the internet routinely that much of the content available emanates from outside the UK and in many instances this does not matter in terms of the user experience.

There is support in general for the view that companies who are relatively new to the audiovisual media services market should be prepared to face some increase in compliance costs. Previously, only broadcasters who were prepared to make significant investments would have been able to offer such services.

Any extension of the Directive would favour large firms who are better able to absorb additional costs of compliance that would arise. It is thought that nothing should be done to encourage the establishment of creative centres outside the EU. The Internet Service Providers Association (ISPA) noted that an obvious compliance cost that would be unwelcome was that arising from pre-transmission monitoring. There is concern that service providers would have to check content before transmission, which could mean editorially reviewing every piece of broadcast type content.

There are also issues around enforcement of the proposed Directive. It is uncertain whether it would be left to the hosting provider to ensure that their customers' broadcasts were within the regulations or whether the hosting providers would be expected to pre-monitor broadcasts. This would generate extortionate costs wholly disproportionate to running the hosting service. Under the E-Commerce Directive (see Chapter 4) hosting providers are free from liability until they are made aware that the material they are hosting is illegal. In addition, internet providers are free from liability for the material they carry over their networks. It is not clear how the proposed changes to the TVWF Directive will be enforced.

Potential for Displacement of Economic Activity

Another issue reviewed by the television and new media industries was the potential for displacement of economic activity as between different parts of the audiovisual services sector or even relocation to non-EU countries.

Might the cost of implementing the Directive be greater than the cost of moving audiovisual ventures outside the EU? If this happened, innovation, investment and employment might well be diverted to non-EU countries. This, in turn, could affect complementary industries dependent on the audiovisual services for their business models, thereby damaging the competitiveness of the EU in the global economy.

Technical advances are such that physical location is increasingly unimportant. A provider of audiovisual services delivered via the internet would have no incentive to locate his or her business in the EU if to do so would subject them to a greater level of regulation, with less editorial and commercial freedom. The UK Film Council commented that so far as film was concerned, they did not believe that any of the options would give rise to decisions to relocate or invest in non-EU locations.

There is some concern that any change could lead to a migration by content owners and advertisers from the more regulated linear services to the less regulated non-linear services.

On the matter of any indirect impact on firms' competitiveness in audiovisual services or more generally, the view of the industry is that European firms' competitiveness is restricted because, with very rare exceptions, European films fare poorly outside their national market. Likewise, European audiovisual service providers rarely operate outside their member state market, let alone outside Europe.

In terms of competitiveness, there is opposition to the proposed imposition of a 35-minute rule for advertising. It is felt that such a rule would not assist organisations working on news and children's programming: rather it would weaken the commercial viability of such programmes.

Country of Origin and Jurisdiction

One very important aspect of the proposed changes to the Directive is the issue of country of origin and jurisdiction.

It is well to remind ourselves that the internet plays havoc with geographical borders and controls. It is important that common treatment of controls in the audiovisual sector exists within the EU, as otherwise competition might be restricted.

The purpose of the TVWF Directive was to create an internal market for television broadcasting through introducing a vital principle – that the country of origin of the broadcaster was the place where media should be regulated, so that programmes could be freely broadcast across borders without reception being blocked within EU countries and that the freedom of speech remained paramount. The country of origin principle is equally important for all information society services and therefore underpins the E-Commerce Directive (see Chapter 4), which now provides the legal framework for the freedom to provide all online media services throughout the EU according to one set of rules.

The television and new media industries have urged the government to resist any amendments designed to weaken the country of origin principle. Arguments for this include the following:

- allowing one member state to regulate an audiovisual media service in another country could lead to undesirable censorship and a restriction of the public's right of access to education, entertainment and information which could result in services and investment relocating outside the EU while continuing to serve markets within the EU;

- companies would not be prepared to launch or run channels if they were subject to varying regulations depending on the country of reception or if the regulatory environment was too uncertain because of new provisions allowing receiving states to complain about services;

- it would be wrong to deny users access to a service that had been approved in another member state and would contravene the principle of free trade within the EU;

- there is a risk that companies would reduce their operations, investment and employment in the UK and that ultimately some might decide to establish themselves outside the UK and probably outside the EU.

In its submission to the consultation process Yahoo! considered that the E-Commerce Directive (see Chapter 4) had provided a sound legal framework within which providers of new media services could flourish. Others felt that the country of origin provisions in the E-Commerce Directive had been effective in overcoming barriers to the free movement of e-commerce services between member states and were a key element in making the single market for services a reality.

The draft Directive includes a new cooperation procedure between national authorities. This will prevent and solve disagreements arising from more restrictive rules existing in a particular member state, in the case of services targeting partially or entirely a territory other than the one of establishment. In the event of failure of this cooperation procedure, it will be up to the Commission to permit possible safeguard measures.

Advertising, Sponsorship and Product Placement

We have already considered the law which applies to online advertising and promotion in this country (Chapter 12). Here we are reviewing the general responses of the television and new media industries to the consultation by the government on the proposed Audiovisual Services Directive on the matter of whether additional advertising control would be required in the context of audiovisual services.

Without advertising revenue many of the films and programmes we enjoy would not get made. At present private TV channels in Europe are reliant on advertising for 90 per cent of their revenue, with the equivalent for public channels being 29 per cent.

Current rules for TV and films guarantee 20 minutes of uninterrupted viewing – except for news, documentaries, religious and children's programmes where, if the entire broadcast is less than 30 minutes, it cannot be interrupted.

The industry felt that the aims of controls on advertising should be supported. However, many feel it is neither appropriate nor necessary to include them in the Directive and there is concern about how they would be interpreted. It is thought that it raises issues of public policy and that the matter was better addressed by general law applicable to all media. It was noted that there are already self-regulating codes and there is also national law and the E-Commerce Directive. A further level of regulation would create legal uncertainty.

Generally, the proposed liberalisation of the rules governing the amount and frequency of advertising allowed on television. There is no support for the proposed '35-minute' rule for advertising breaks in films, news and children's programmes.

In the 1980s advertisers began to fear that advertising overkill was having the opposite effect. People were turning off advertisements. A popular solution has been product placement, where the main characters drink, drive or collect whatever the sponsors tell them to. The recent James Bond Film *Casino Royale* continued the Bond tradition of the hero having a strong affinity with certain cars.

The proposal to allow isolated advertising and teleshopping spots in sports programmes while making them the exception in other programmes is generally felt to be beneficial in so far as it would create additional opportunities for broadcasters to generate revenue from advertising.

The general approach likely to be adopted for advertising mainly follows the Commission proposal. For programme types which are specifically protected, such as cinematographic works or television films, the compromise permits the possibility of an interruption every 30 minutes instead of the 35 proposed by the Commission.

Concerning product placement, there is a prohibition in principle, from which each member state will be able to derogate explicitly. Member states can authorise product placement in drama and entertainment programmes, but under no circumstances in children's programmes.

Bibliography

Cornthwaite, J. (2000). *The Internet and Intellectual Property*, 2nd ed. Sudbury: Monitor Press.

Department For Culture, Media and Sport (2006). Consultation on the proposal by the European Commission for the revision of the Television Without Frontiers Directive. December.

Gates, W.H. with N. Myhrvold and P. Rinearson (1995). *The Road Ahead*. New York: Viking Penguin.

Gringras, C. (2002). *The Laws of the Internet*, 2nd ed. London: Butterworths.

Harrison, A. (2003). *Music: The Business – The Essential Guide to the Law and the Deals*, 2nd ed. London: Virgin Books.

Mosawi, A. (1997). *Entertainment Law: a Guide to Contracts in the Film Industry*. London: Butterworths.

Nwakodo, R. and S. Singleton (2005). *E-Contracts*. Haywards Heath: Tottel Publishing Ltd.

Sparrow, A. (2004). *The Law of Internet and Mobile Communications – The EU and US Contrasted*. Harley, Shrewsbury: tfm Publishing Ltd.

Sparrow, A. (2001). *The E Commerce Handbook*. London: Fitzwarren Handbooks.

Sparrow, A. (2006) *Music Distribution and the Internet – A Legal Guide For The Music Business*. Aldershot: Gower Publishing.

Stowe, K. (2005). *Distance Selling Changes*. E Commerce Law and Policy. August. 7:8.

Index

If you have found this book useful you may be interested in the companion volume

Music Distribution and the Internet: A Legal Guide for the Music Business
Andrew Sparrrow
0 566 08709 X

There is hardly an aspect of internet music promotion, sale and distribution which does not have a legal dimension. Since the stakeholders in the process includes artists, their managers, music publishers, record companies, distribution companies and the consumer, the law relating to internet music distribution is extremely complex.

Andrew Sparrow's Music Distribution and the Internet provides those connected to the music and media industries with a guide to the legal requirements they must meet, answering questions such as:

• How should you conclude contracts with consumers over the internet?
• What are the various legal terms and conditions that should govern the sale of physical product to online music buyers?
• How should a website user's personal information be handled?
• What limitations are there on the way this data may be used for ongoing marketing of an artist's work or the merchandise associated with it?
• What are the latest copyright laws in this area and how do they apply to the internet?

The book provides practical advice on how to approach key relationships with the internet buying consumer and other online media providers. The law is explained in straightforward terms and applied throughout in a music business context.

Music Distribution and the Internet is an essential reference for anyone seeking to exploit and protect their rights and those of their artists in the rapidly expanding, constantly evolving and fascinating arena that is new media.

For further information on this and all our titles visit our website – www.gowerpub.com
All online orders receive a discount

GOWER

Join our e-mail newsletter

Gower is widely recognized as one of the world's leading publishers on management and business practice. Its programmes range from 1000-page handbooks through practical manuals to popular paperbacks. These cover all the main functions of management: human resource development, sales and marketing, project management, finance, etc. Gower also produces training videos and activities manuals on a wide range of management skills.

As our list is constantly developing you may find it difficult to keep abreast of new titles. With this in mind we offer a free e-mail news service, approximately once every two months, which provides a brief overview of the most recent titles and links into our catalogue, should you wish to read more or see sample pages.

To sign up to this service, send your request via e-mail to info@gowerpub.com. Please put your e-mail address in the body of the e-mail as confirmation of your agreement to receive information in this way.

GOWER